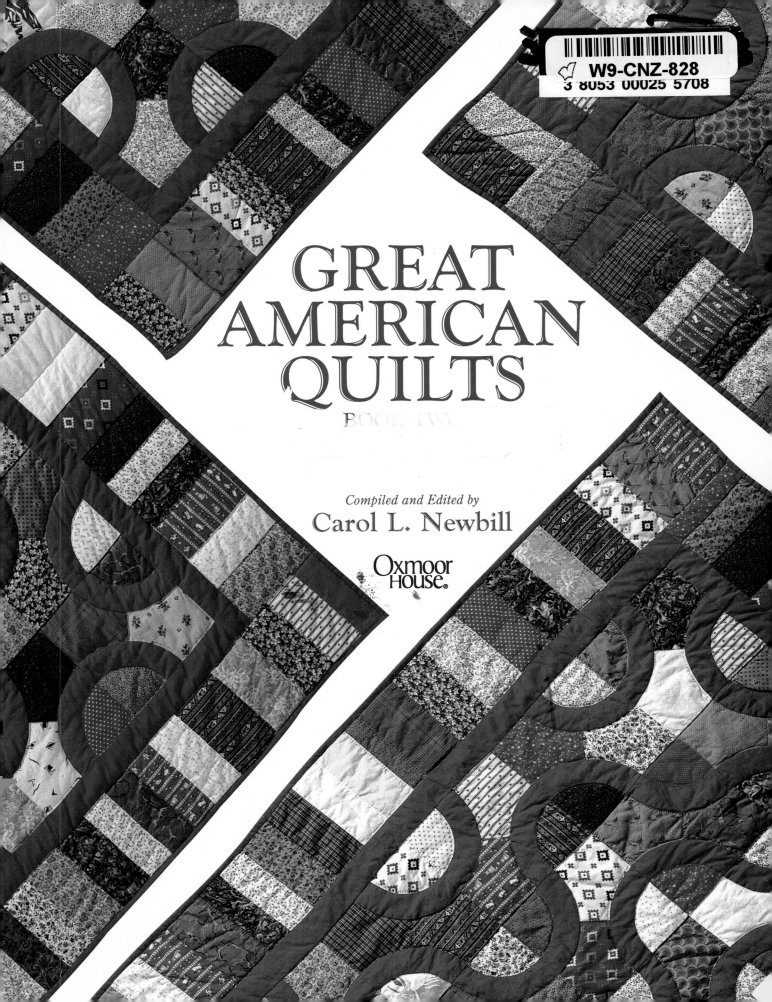

GREAT AMERICAN QUILTS

BOOK TWO

Compiled and Edited by
Carol L. Newbill

Oxmoor
House

Great American Quilts Book Two

Published by Oxmoor House, Inc., and Leisure Arts, Inc.

Library of Congress Catalog Number: 86-62283
ISBN: 0-8487-1401-6
ISSN: 1076-7673
Manufactured in the United States of America
Second Printing 1995

Editor-in-Chief: Nancy J. Fitzpatrick
Senior Crafts Editor: Susan Ramey Wright
Senior Editor, Editorial Services: Olivia Kindig Wells
Art Director: James Boone

Great American Quilts Book Two

Editor: Carol Logan Newbill
Assistant Editor: Catherine S. Corbett
Editorial Assistant: Jennifer K. Mathews
Copy Editor: Susan Smith Cheatham
Production and Distribution Director: Phillip Lee
Production Manager: Gail Morris
Associate Production Manager: Theresa L. Beste
Production Assistant: Marianne Jordan
Designer: Eleanor Cameron
Patterns and Illustrations: Kelly Davis
Senior Photographer: John O'Hagan
Photostylist: Katie Stoddard

Additional photography: Roy Dankman (pages 134, 144)

Cover quilt: *Roads*, by Becky Olson Johnson (page18)

EDITOR'S NOTE

This year, the topic for our special chapter is "Circles and Curves." Leading the way is a quilt from Pepper Cory, well-known teacher, author, and tireless promoter of the Drunkard's Path pattern. Pepper's quilt, *Flying Under Radar,* is a Drunkard's Path variation she uses when teaching that also incorporates very special memories. Read its story on page 8.

What do quilting and crystallography have in common? More than you might think. Look at Cora Hartley's striking geometric *Cool and Bold* to find out how you can make circles from diamond-shaped templates. Or enjoy Martha Skelton's fresh update of a 1930s block in *Flower Reel.*

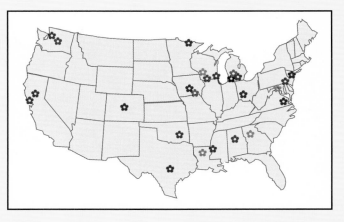

Star patterns, a perennial favorite of quilters, show up in both "Traditions" and "Quilts Across America" this year! From Judith Hindall's *Starlight Nights-Garden Delights,* sure to charm any quilter who loves cats, to Fern Stewart's *Southwestern Star* and Barbara Tricarico's *Vienna Stars,* a starstruck quilter of any skill level can find a pleasing pattern here.

If you're a Christmas quilt lover, be sure to see Carol Butzke's *Visions of Santa Danced in My Head* and the Wenonah Depot Quilters' *Cottages in the Snow.* Try combining the two patterns into one quilt for a special holiday wall hanging, or make a set of place mats for your table using the different blocks.

One very special quilt to those of us at Oxmoor House is on page 124. *There's No Place Like Oxmoor House* is a quilt designed and made by former Oxmoor House editor Barbara Abrelat from friendship blocks made for her by members of our editorial staff. In "Designer Gallery," you'll see another of Barbara's quilts, *City of Gold,* made to celebrate the 1996 Summer Olympics to be held in Atlanta, Georgia.

Enjoy the quilts these 28 talented quiltmakers have shared with you this year!

Where do our Great American quilters come from? They come from Pennsylvania and Washington, from Minnesota and Mississippi, from Virginia and from Iowa. This year's book features quilts from quilters and quilting groups in 17 different states across America.

If your state isn't represented, let us put a star on next year's map for you! For information on submitting a quilt, write to *Great American Quilts* Editor, Oxmoor House, 2100 Lakeshore Drive, Birmingham, AL 35209.

CONTENTS

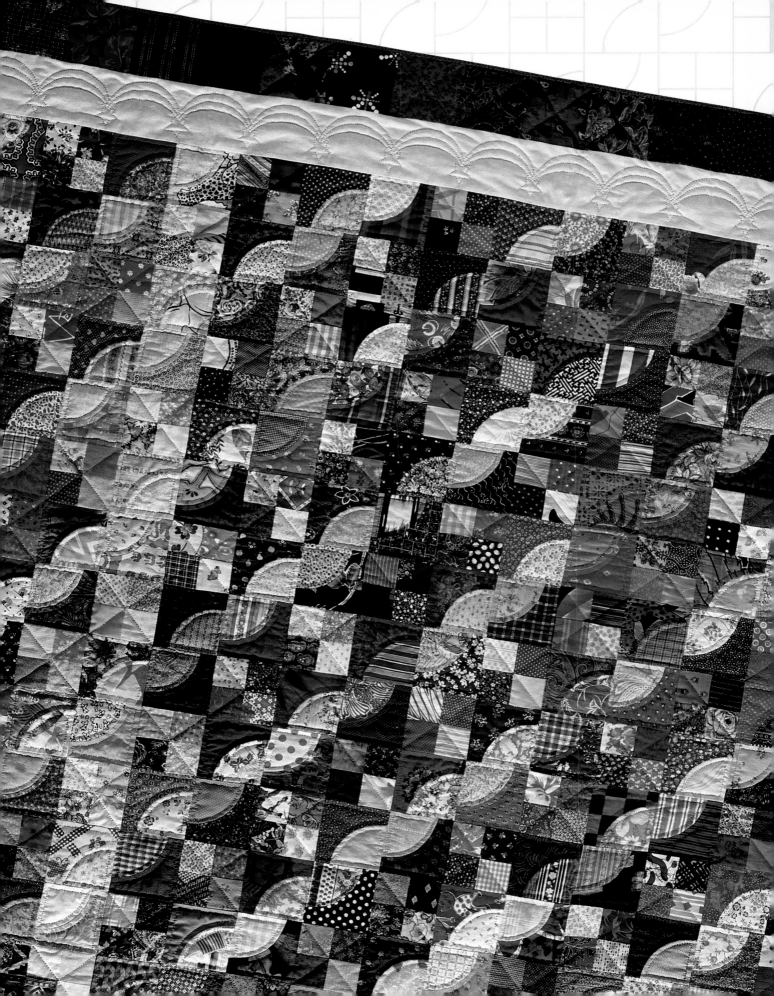

CIRCLES & CURVES

"I remain fascinated with why people choose to learn quilting, how they use quilting in their lives as a bridge to communicate with others."

Pepper Cory
LANSING, MICHIGAN

"I f what you are doing is so important that you want it on your headstone, then it's important enough to make time for." This is the philosophy Pepper Cory espouses for quilters trying to juggle homes, careers, and quilting. With a twinkle, she asks, "Do you *really* want people to remember you for keeping the cleanest bathroom in town?"

The past decade has seen Pepper focus her energies on writing and teaching. She travels extensively to teach and is the author of several books, including *Happy Trails,* a book devoted to the many possibilities presented by the Drunkard's Path pattern. She also writes articles for quilting magazines and designs a line of quilting stencils.

With all of the demands on her time, what does Pepper consider the most important activity in her life? "My husband has instructions," she says with a smile, "in case I predecease him, to put 'Quilter' on my headstone."

Flying Under Radar
1994

"I thought I'd never be one to make a charm quilt," Pepper says, "since they require so many fabrics, and I thought that piecing only one template might be boring." But two incidents combined to change her mind: the formation of the Daughters of Charm, a subgroup of the Capitol City Quilt Guild devoted to making charm quilts, and the publication of an article that suggested that the one-template limitation was a guideline, not a rule. "The members exchanged 5" squares of fabric in

previously agreed-upon colors," Pepper says. "We were supposed to wait until we had exchanged all the fabrics before beginning, but I was so impatient to start that I began working the first week. I added blocks as I got each group of fabrics, so the waves of color naturally grew in an L-fashion."

The majority of *Flying UnderRadar* was pieced during the winter of 1990–1991. "Like most of America, I was engrossed by the Gulf War. As I watched and listened," Pepper

says, "the quilt took on an unexpected meaning for me. The Stealth airplanes I was seeing on TV were somehow related to the winged images emerging from the quilt, and I was reminded of my father, a World War II pilot, and his experiences flying 'under radar' in northern Italy. This quilt has evolved into a memorial quilt to my father and to all other pilots, known and unknown, who flew under radar."

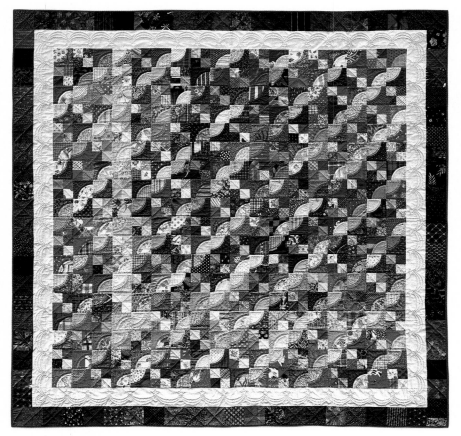

Flying Under Radar

Finished Quilt Size
88" x 88"

Number of Blocks and Finished Size
216 Drunkard's Path blocks	4" x 4"
108 Four-patch blocks	4" x 4"

Fabric Requirements
Off-white	2¼ yards
Assorted light prints	3 yards
Assorted dark prints	3 yards
Backing	8 yards
Red for bias binding	1 yard

Pieces to Cut
Off-white
2 (4½" x 72½") border strips
2 (4½" x 80½") border strips
Assorted light prints
216 B
216 C
Assorted dark prints
216 A
216 C
84 D

Quilt Top Assembly
1. Following Drunkard's Path Block Assembly Diagram, join 1 dark print A and 1 light print B to make 1 Drunkard's Path block. (Refer to Quilt Smart, "Piecing Curves," on page 12 for more information.) Repeat to make 216 Drunkard's Path blocks.

Following Four-patch Block Assembly Diagram, join 2 light print Cs and 2 dark print Cs to make 1 Four-patch block. Repeat to make 108 Four-patch blocks.

Pepper's father, Joseph Scott Peddie, who died in 1985, was an Air Force pilot assigned to Intelligence and stationed in North Africa and Italy during World War II. His assignment was to keep track of the locations of Allied prisoner of war camps, so that the Allied pilots could avoid them during bombing runs. But Peddie and other Intelligence pilots began to fly clandestine missions into northern Italy and Germany, often in tiny two-seater Piper Cubs, dropping Allied intelligence agents and picking them up before the enemy forces advanced. To avoid detection, the pilots had to fly at low altitudes—literally "under radar"—sometimes so low that leaves and tree branches were stuck in the airplane's undercarriage upon returning.

"My father died before the Gulf War began," Pepper says. "I often wonder what he would have thought of the Stealth airplanes—planes that radar couldn't detect."

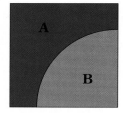

Drunkard's Path Assembly Diagram

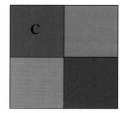

Four-Patch Block Assembly Diagram

On the back, Pepper added this unusual documentation block, a perfect complement to the quilt.

2. For each row, refer to photograph for color placement and join 12 Drunkard's Path blocks and 6 Four-patch blocks as shown in Quilt Top Assembly Diagram. Make 18 rows; join rows.

3. Join 4½" x 72½" off-white border strips to top and bottom of quilt. Join 4½" x 80½" off-white border strips to sides of quilt, butting corners.

4. To make top pieced border, join 20 dark print Ds; join to top of quilt. Repeat to make bottom border; join to bottom of quilt. To make 1 side

pieced border, join 22 Ds; repeat to make second side pieced border. Join to sides of quilt, butting corners.

Quilting
Quilt As, Bs, Cs, and Ds in-the-ditch or ¼" inside seam line; or quilt as desired. Quilt star-and-swag pattern (see "Resources") in off-white border, or quilt border as desired.

Finished Edges
Bind with bias binding made from red fabric.

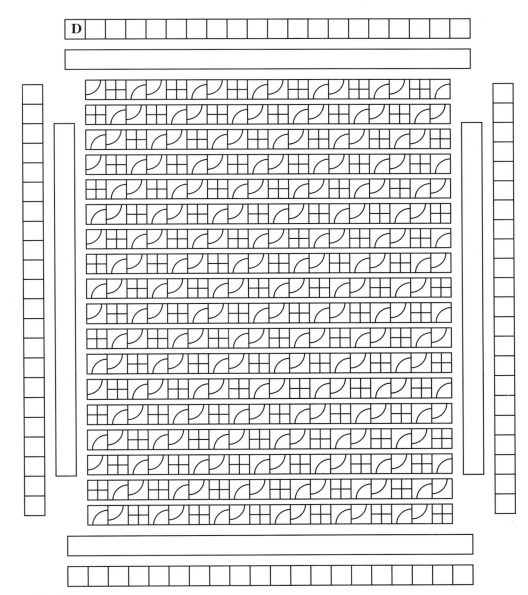

Quilt Top Assembly Diagram

❖ Quilt Smart

Piecing Curves

Method 1: Piecing curves on your machine doesn't have to be difficult, but it does require a little extra care to ensure accurate seams. Following Figure 1, first mark the centers of both the convex (outward) and concave (inward) curves. Then sew a line of stay-stitching just inside the seam allowance of both pieces. Carefully clip the seam allowance of the concave piece to the stay-stitching.

With right sides facing and ends and centers aligned, pin the two curved patches together at the center (Figure 2) and the left edge (Figure 3). Carefully sew from the end to the center, stopping frequently to check that the raw edges are aligned. Stop at the center with your needle down. Raise the presser foot and pin the pieces together from the center to the right edge. Lower the presser foot and continue to sew from the center to the right edge, checking frequently as above. Press the seam toward the concave curve (Figure 4).

Method 2: Another method sometimes used for piecing Drunkard's Path blocks takes a bit more time but produces a smooth, perfect curve on each seam.

Begin by making a pressing template for piece B from Templar (a heat-resistant, translucent nylon sheet available from quilting shops) or from a lightweight aluminum sheet such as the bottom of a disposable pie pan. (This is a good excuse to buy—and eat— a ready-to-bake pie!) Referring to Figure 5, cut the pressing template so that it includes seam allowances along the straight sides but *does not* include the seam allowance along the curve.

Place the fabric piece B, right side down, on the ironing board. Dampen the curved section with water or spray starch. Place the pressing template on the fabric, aligning the straight edges (Figure 6). Using the tip of the iron, press the curved seam allowance back over the pressing template. If you are using an aluminum template, make sure to keep your fingers about 1" to 1½" away from the iron; the metal becomes uncomfortably warm only at the pressed edge. When the seam allowance is dry, carefully remove the template.

Place piece B on piece A, right sides up and aligning seam lines; pin (Figure 7). Now stitch the seam, using one of these methods.

1. Topstitch (Figure 8), using matching or contrasting thread.

2. Machine-blindstitch, using nylon monofilament ("invisible" thread) or matching or contrasting thread (Figure 9).

3. Hand-blindstitch, using matching thread (Figure 10). This results in an almost invisible seam.

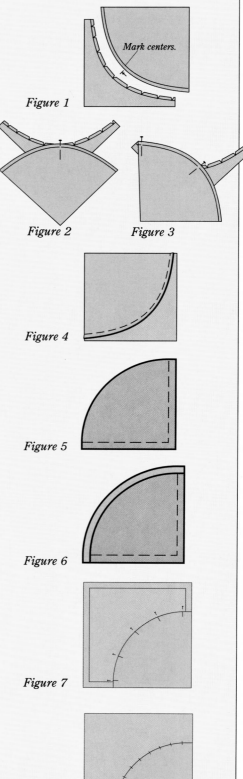

Figure 1

Figure 2 *Figure 3*

Figure 4

Figure 5

Figure 6

Figure 7

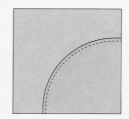

Figure 8

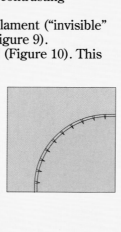

Figure 9

Figure 10

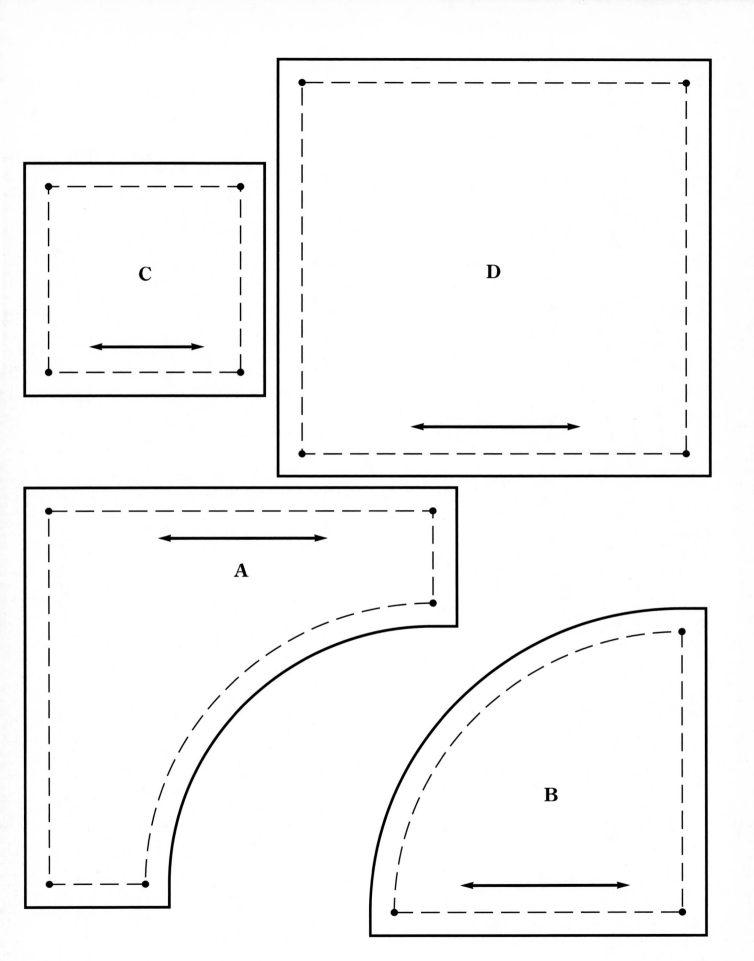

"I began with the center of the quilt and worked out and around. I didn't plan to make it circular until I discovered that I didn't have enough of one of the fabrics!"

Cora B. Hartley
MANSON, WASHINGTON

A professional singer, former professor of music, pianist, church organist, music teacher, and accomplished quilter, Cora Hartley is certainly multitalented. Cora says that her lifelong fascination with both music and quilting stems from memories of her grandmother, who taught her to play the piano. When Cora was not practicing music, she would sit beside her grandmother and watch her make quilts or would admire and arrange the various scraps of colorful fabric.

While Cora's interest in music developed into a career, her love of quilts became an impressive hobby. She began quilting almost 40 years ago and has completed nearly one new quilt each month, for an impressive total of 447—and counting! Active in her community and in quiltmaking, she says she is "loving every minute" of her busy life.

Cool and Bold
1992

What do quilting and physics have in common? More than you might think. Cora was fascinated with this design, which was discovered by her friend Robert L. Ingalls, a University of Washington physics professor. The pattern occurs in the crystalline structure of some metal mixes. It is unusual in both the worlds of quilting and crystallography because it has 10 units (diamonds to quilters, "rhombs" to scientists) around the center rather than the usual 6 or 8 units. Cora volunteered to make a quilt for Dr. Ingalls from his design. When asked which colors he preferred, he replied that his favorite colors were "cool and bold." Using bright turquoise fabric and only three templates, she combined the beauty of quilts and crystals.

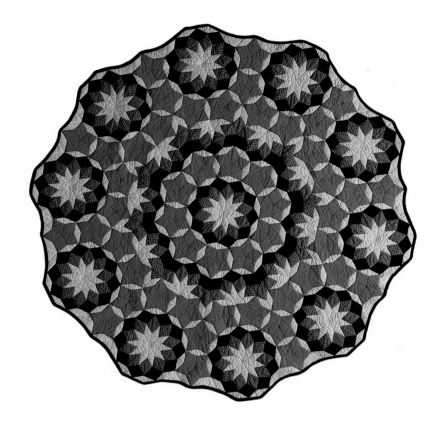

Block 1 Diagram—Make 11.

Turquoise Star Diagram—Make 50.

Print Star Diagram—Make 10.

Flower Diagram—Make 10.

Cool and Bold

Finished Quilt Size
74" diameter

Fabric Requirements

White	3½ yards
Turquoise solid	3 yards
Turquoise print	2 yards
Black	1¾ yards
Backing	4½ yards
Black for bias binding	1 yard

Pieces to Cut

White	380 A
	20 C
Turquoise solid	250 B
Turquoise print	160 B
Black	140 B

Quilt Top Assembly

1. Referring to Block 1 Diagram, join 20 white As, 10 turquoise print Bs, and 10 black Bs to make 1 Block 1. Repeat to make 11 Block 1s.

2. Referring to Turquoise Star Diagram, join 5 turquoise solid Bs to make 1 turquoise star. Repeat to make 50 turquoise stars.

3. Referring to Print Star Diagram, join 2 black Bs and 3 turquoise print Bs to make 1 print star. Repeat to make 10 print stars.

4. Referring to Flower Diagram, join 5 white As, 2 turquoise print Bs, and 1 black B to make 1 flower. Repeat to make 10 flowers.

5. Following Quilt Top Assembly Diagram and referring to "Set-in Seams" on page 17, join Block 1s, turquoise stars, print stars, and flowers with remaining white As and Cs.

Quilting
Quilt each diamond in-the-ditch, or quilt as desired.

Finished Edges
Bind with bias binding made from black.

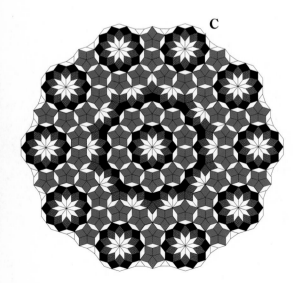

Quilt Top Assembly Diagram

❖ Quilt Smart

Set-in Seams

Because each piece in *Cool and Bold* is a diamond or a triangle, most of the seams used to join the pieces will require sewing into an angle (Figure 1). Although many quilters feel that set-in seams must be pieced by hand, successful corners can be sewn by machine as well.

Follow these steps to be sure that the seams meet smoothly, no matter which method you use.

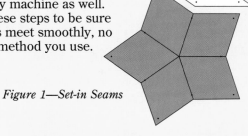

Figure 1—Set-in Seams

1. On the wrong side of each piece, mark corner dots. If you plan to piece by hand, you may also find it helpful to mark all seam lines.

2. With right sides facing, pin first 2 diamonds together, matching dots. Stitch from dot to dot, backstitching (if sewing by machine) or knotting thread (if sewing by hand) to secure ends of seam. Finger-press seam to one side.

3. With right sides facing, pin third diamond to 1 edge of 1 joined diamond, matching dots (Figure 2). Beginning at inner corner, stitch to outer dot. Backstitch or knot ends of thread.

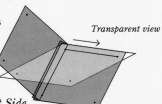

Transparent view

Figure 2—Attaching 1st Side

4. With right sides facing, pin adjacent raw edge of third diamond to edge of remaining diamond, matching dots (Figure 3). Beginning again at inner corner, stitch to outer dot. Backstitch or knot ends of thread. Trim seam allowances at inner corners to reduce bulk.

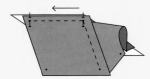

Figure 3—Attaching 2nd Side

5. To press seam, swirl seam allowances as shown (Figure 4). Press or finger-press seams to one side for a smooth, finished seam (Figure 5).

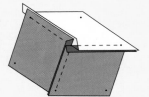

Figure 4—Pressing Guide

Figure 5—Finished Seam

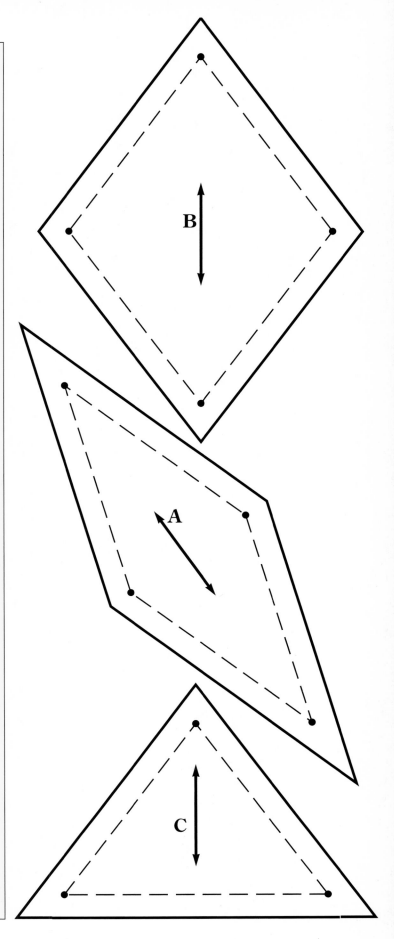

Becky Olson Johnson
BADGER, MINNESOTA

Becky Johnson has been quilting since 1988 and in that time has finished "too many quilts to count." As the owner of a quilt shop, she has used much of her work as class samples or store models to assist other quilters in selecting colors or learning a particular technique.

When asked which of the many techniques she prefers, Becky answers "All of them! I teach hand and machine piecing, hand and machine appliqué, machine quilting, and rotary cutting without templates. My favorite part of quilting may be playing with the fabric and planning how the quilt will go together, but piecing the quilt top is also exciting. As you complete each step, the results of your planning become apparent."

Roads
1990

Becky made *Roads* as a gift for her nephew, Matthew, who chose the pattern from a book. "It seemed appropriate for Matthew," Becky says, "because he loves to play with toy cars, and the blue arcs make perfect roads for his vehicles. Also, it reminds him of his Aunt Becky, who is always 'on the road.' So far, I have lived in nine states and in Amsterdam, but I hope that my recent move back home to Minnesota is the last."

Quilt Top Assembly

1. Join 1 light print A to 1 dark print A along short edges as shown in Block Assembly Diagram. Join 1 light print B to 1 C; join 1 dark print B to 1 C. Join to As as shown to complete 1 block. Repeat to make 60 blocks.

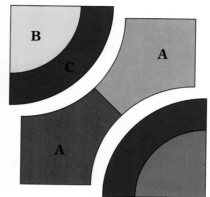

Block Assembly Diagram

2. Following Quilt Top Assembly Diagram for placement, join blocks in 10 rows of 6 blocks each. Be careful to orient each block as shown to create the "road" pattern. Join rows.

3. Join 2¼" x 80½" blue solid border strips to sides of quilt top. Join 2¼" x 52" blue solid border strips to top and bottom of quilt top, butting corners.

4. To make 1 pieced side border, join 31 (3" x 6½") print strips along long edges, alternating dark and light prints as shown in photograph. Join 1 (3½" x 6½") print strip to each end of pieced border. Repeat to make second side border. Join pieced borders to sides of quilt top.

To make top pieced border, join 23 (3" x 6½") print strips along long edges, alternating dark and light prints as shown in photograph. Join 1 (3½" x 6½") print strip to each end of pieced border. Repeat to make bottom border. Join pieced borders to top and bottom of quilt top, butting corners.

Quilting

Quilt each seam in-the-ditch, or quilt as desired.

Finished Edges

Bind with bias binding made from blue solid.

Roads

Finished Quilt Size
63½" x 95½"

Number of Blocks and Finished Size
60 blocks   8" x 8"

Fabric Requirements
Blue solid	2¾ yards
Assorted light prints	3 yards
Assorted dark prints	3 yards
Backing	5¾ yards
Blue solid for bias binding	1 yard

Pieces to Cut
Blue solid
   2 (2¼" x 80½") border strips
   2 (2¼" x 52") border strips
   120 C
Assorted light prints
   54 (3" x 6½") border strips
   4 (3½" x 6½") border strips
   60 A
   60 B
Assorted dark prints
   54 (3" x 6½") border strips
   4 (3½" x 6½") border strips
   60 A
   60 B

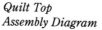

Quilt Top Assembly Diagram

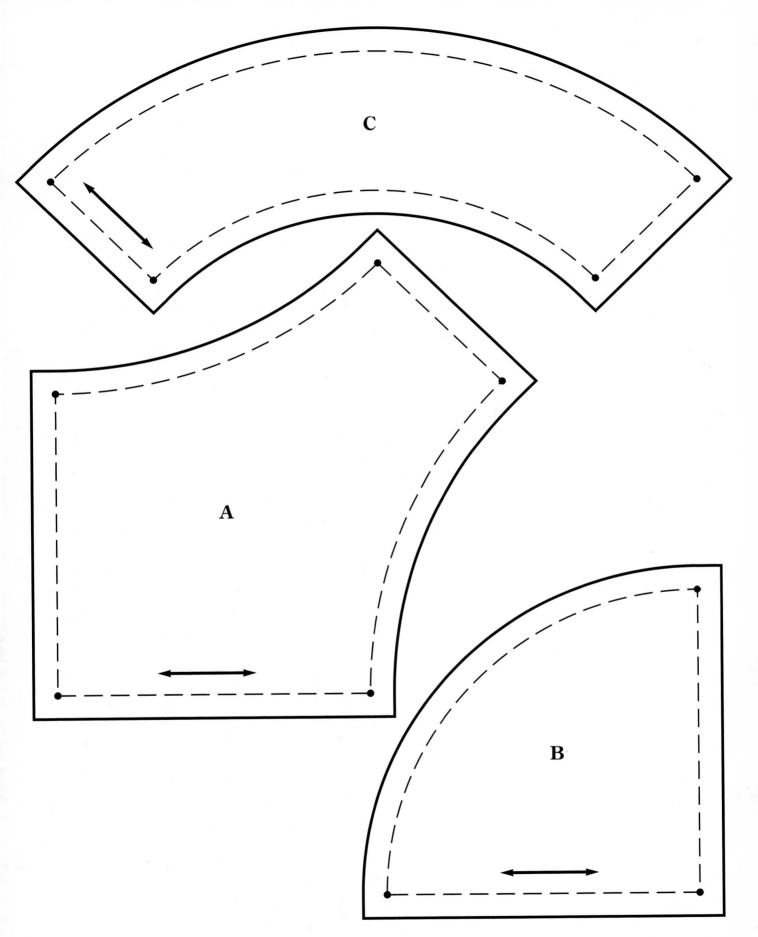

"It took me four years to complete Whispering Leaves, *but I completed my master's degree at the same time!"*

Ginny Bauhof
KALAMAZOO, MICHIGAN

"I love to quilt," Ginny Bauhof says, "but I am probably one of the *least* prolific members of my guild, the Log Cabin Quilters." That she has little time to quilt is not surprising; Ginny is a full-time professor at Western Michigan University and has three children at home. Despite the demands on her time, she has completed a number of small pieces as well as two large quilts, and she especially enjoys making friendship blocks for those in her guild.

"It really encourages me to grow as a quilter when I deal with color, shading, and technique to please another quilter," she says. "Making friendship blocks has certainly improved my skills because I've tried things I might not otherwise have tried, and I even ended up liking things I thought I wouldn't!"

Whispering Leaves
1986

The dark green fabric Ginny used in *Whispering Leaves* is a cherished favorite. "I bought several yards of the fabric when I was a teenager sewing my own clothes," Ginny says, "but I never found a dress pattern I liked well enough to cut into it." About 10 years ago, she saw a red-and-white quilt similar to *Whispering Leaves* in a local quilt show and decided that if she ever made a large quilt, she would use that pattern and the green fabric. "I had a bad moment when I unfolded it to cut the pieces and found that it was only 36" wide!" Ginny says. Fortunately, the amount she had bought to make a dress was enough to finish the quilt.

Ginny credits a good friend and fellow quiltmaker with encouraging her, as a relative newcomer to quilting, to make a large quilt. "I had made several small pieces," she says, "and my friend kept urging me to start the big quilt. I'm forever grateful that her 'nagging' got me over the hurdle of beginning."

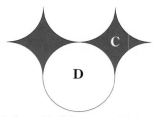

Block 2 Assembly Diagram—Make 8.

Whispering Leaves

Finished Quilt Size
80½" x 96"

Fabric Requirements
White	6 yards
Dark green	2½ yards
Light green	3¾ yards
Backing	5¾ yards
Dark green for bias binding	1 yard

Pieces to Cut
White
  2 (9½" x 59") border strips
  2 (11½" x 96½") border strips
  100 A
  8 D
Dark green
  2 (4" x 81") appliquéd border
    strips
  2 (4" x 78½") appliquéd border
    strips
  200 B
Light green
  130 C

Quilt Top Assembly
1. Referring to Block 1 Assembly Diagram, join 2 As, 4 Bs, and 2 Cs to make 1 Block 1. Repeat to make 50 Block 1s.

Referring to Block 2 Assembly Diagram, join 2 Cs and 1 D to make 1 Block 2. Repeat to make 8 Block 2s.

See Quilt Smart, "Piecing Tips," on page 27 for information on joining curved seams.

2. On large surface or design wall (see Quilt Smart on page 37), arrange Cs, Ds, and blocks as shown in Quilt Top Assembly Diagram. Join all pieces.

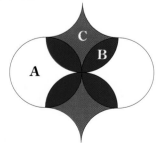

Block 1 Assembly Diagram—Make 50.

3. To attach top border, place right side of 1 (9½" x 59") white border strip facing wrong side of top row. Align seam line of border strip with center line of Cs, as shown in Border Assembly Diagram. Baste quilt top to border along seam line. Appliqué raw edges of Cs to border strip. Remove basting stitches. Repeat to attach bottom border.

Attach 11½" x 96½" white border strips to sides of quilt top in same manner, butting corners.

4. To complete scalloped outer edge of border, place 1 (4" x 81") dark green strip along top edge of quilt, with right sides facing up and raw edges aligned. Baste dark green strip to border, stitching ¼" to ½" from raw edges. Place and baste remaining 4" x 81" strip along bottom edge of quilt in same manner. Place and baste 4" x 78½" dark green strips along sides of quilt top.

Referring to Scallop Placement Diagram and using corner and scallop guides, transfer scalloped edges to dark green border strips. Cut dark green strips along marked scallop lines, being careful not to cut underlying white border. Appliqué raw edges to white border.

Quilting
Quilt Palm Quilting Pattern in As, Ds, and along white borders, following photograph for placement. Quilt in-the-ditch around Bs and appliquéd scallops in border. Quilt Cs ¼" inside seam line.

Finished Edges
Bind with bias binding made from dark green fabric.

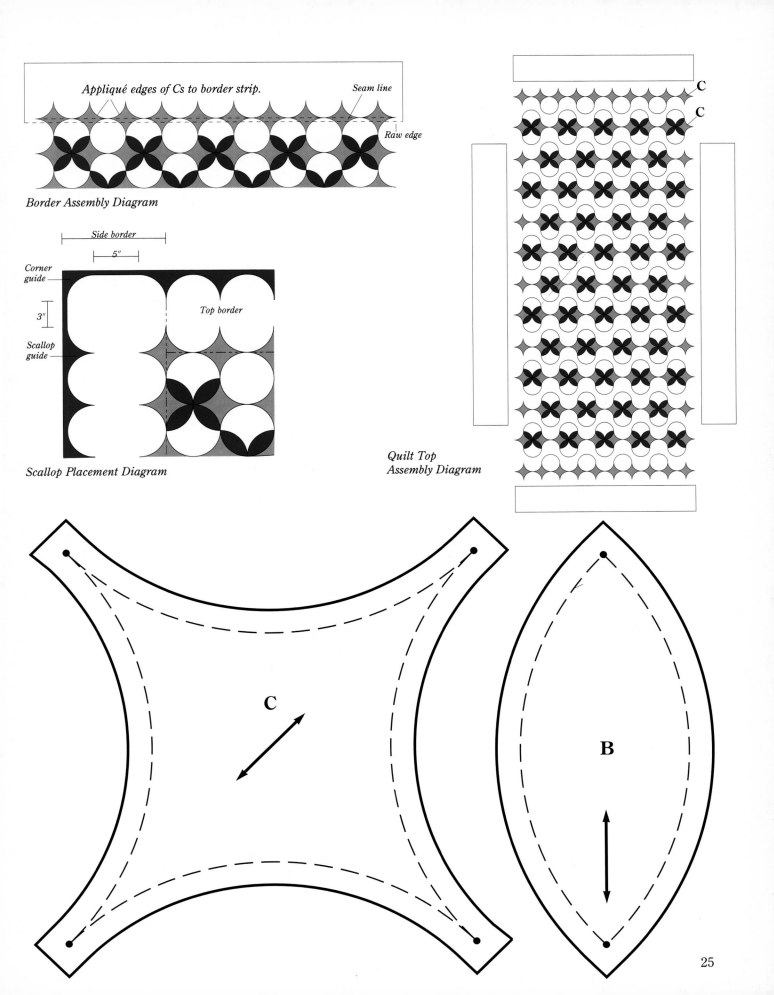

Appliqué edges of Cs to border strip.

Seam line

Raw edge

Border Assembly Diagram

Side border

5"

Corner guide

3"

Top border

Scallop guide

Scallop Placement Diagram

C
C

Quilt Top
Assembly Diagram

C

B

25

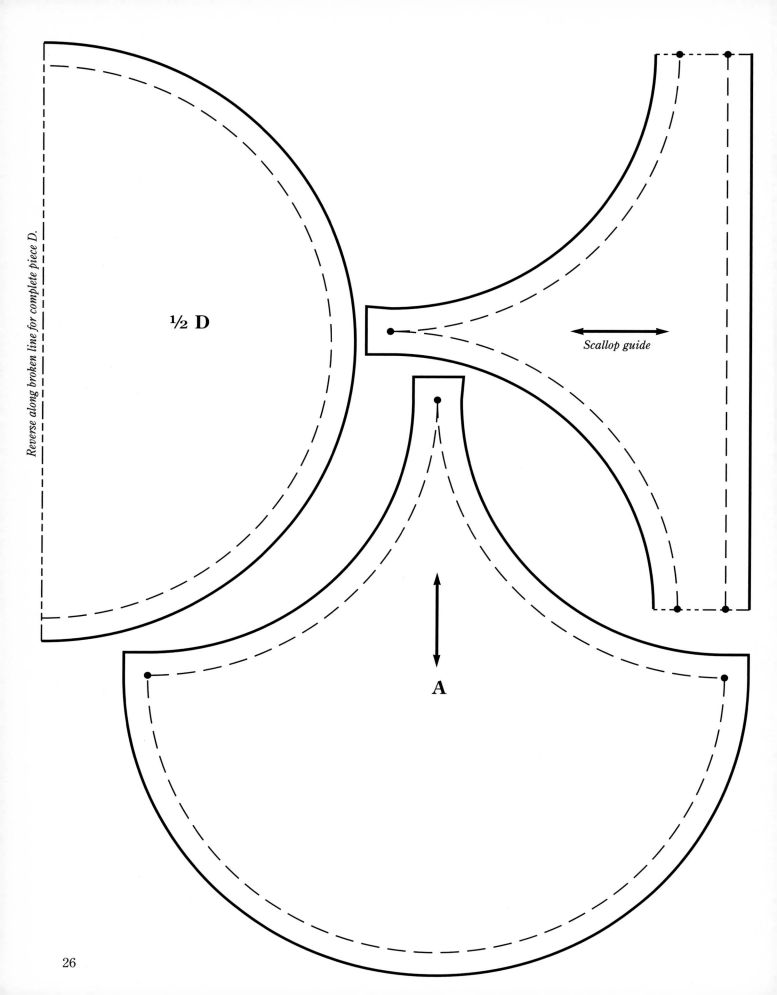

½ **D**

Reverse along broken line for complete piece D.

Scallop guide

A

❖ Quilt Smart

Piecing Tips

General instructions for machine-piecing quarter-circle curves are given on page 12 for *Flying Under Radar,* a variation of Drunkard's Path. In addition to those instructions, here are some tips to help make piecing *Whispering Leaves* easier.

1. When making Block 1s, join 2 Bs to 1 A; repeat. Then join Cs to complete block. In this way, you will never be faced with a seam that is longer than one-fourth of the circle.

2. Even if the curve is continuous, as when joining Cs and Ds for Block 2s and when joining completed blocks, don't try to stitch more than one-fourth of a circle at a time. Plan to break your stitching at these points so that you can more easily align and pin the next section for stitching.

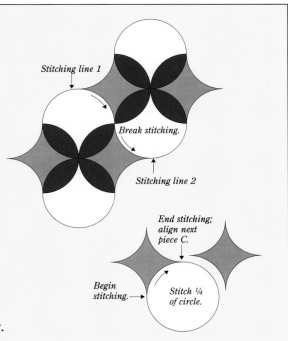

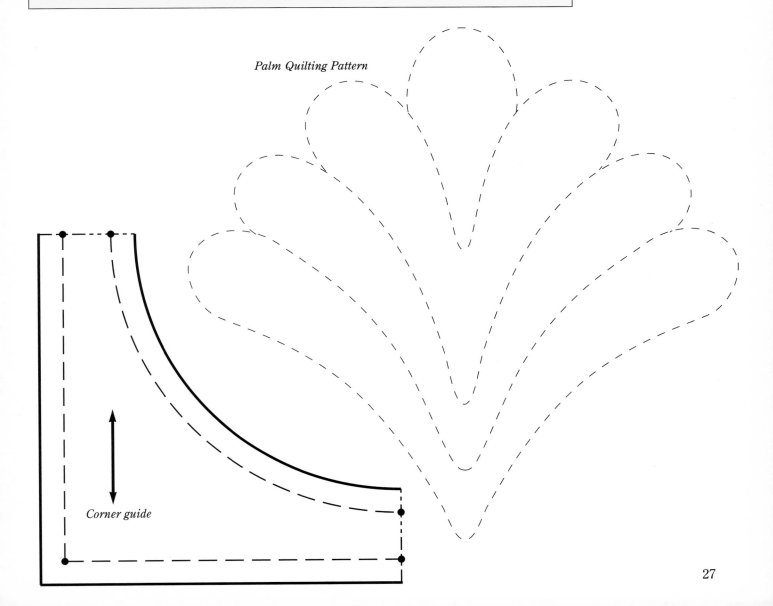

Palm Quilting Pattern

Corner guide

"I've met people through my quilting who have added so much to my life. Quilts are meant to be shared."

Martha Skelton
VICKSBURG, MISSISSIPPI

Nationally recognized for her design skills and impeccable workmanship, Martha Skelton has been making beautiful quilts for most of her life. "I come from people who like to do things with their hands," Martha says. "I learned quilting from my mother and grandmother, but all my family—and friends as well—quilted." Two of Martha's quilts are part of the permanent collection of the Museum of The American Quilter's Society in Paducah, Kentucky. Others have been shown in special exhibits in the Netherlands and in Germany. Despite the many awards and accolades she has received, Martha says that the most satisfying part of showing her quilts and teaching quiltmaking is meeting people from all walks of life.

Flower Reel
1988

Flower Reel is Martha's adaptation of a pattern called Posies Round the Square, originally published in *Needlecrafts/The Home Art Magazine* in 1934. She saw a quilt made from this pattern in a 1978 magazine, but that quilt used a limited color range and a straight block setting. Martha designed the quilt setting to show off her flawless quilting and added the border in bright floral colors to complement the blocks.

"I made *Flower Reel* for my granddaughter, Jennifer," Martha says. "By using these colors, I hoped to give her a quilt she would enjoy over a long period of time."

Flower Reel won the Viewers' Choice award at the 1988 Vicksburg Cotton Patchers quilt show and was featured in the 1989 Engagement Calendar published by The American Quilter's Society.

Flower Reel

Finished Quilt Size
72" x 87¼"

Number of Blocks and Finished Size
22 blocks   11" x 11"

Fabric Requirements

White	5¼ yards
Assorted yellow prints	1½ yards or 6 fat quarters
Assorted blue prints	1½ yards or 6 fat quarters
Assorted lavender prints	1¼ yards or 5 fat quarters
Assorted pink prints	1¼ yards or 5 fat quarters
Green print	¾ yard
Yellow solid	¼ yard
Backing	5¼ yards
White for bias binding	1 yard

Pieces to Cut
White
 10 (11½") setting squares
 4 (16¾") squares*
 2 (8¾") squares**
 22 A
 88 C
 62 G

Assorted yellow prints
 24 B†
 24 D†
 15 H
 6 I
Assorted blue prints
 24 B†
 24 D†
 14 H
 3 I
Assorted lavender prints
 20 B†
 20 D†
 15 H
 1 I
Assorted pink prints
 20 B†
 20 D†
 14 H
 2 I
Green print
 176 F
Yellow solid
 88 E

*Cut each square into quarters diagonally; discard 2 for 14 side triangles.
**Cut each square in half diagonally for 4 corner triangles.
†Cut 4 Bs and 4 Ds from each print.

Quilt Top Assembly
1. Following Block Assembly Diagram, join 4 Bs of same print to 1 A. To 1 C, appliqué 1 D of same print as Bs. Appliqué 1 E to center of D. Appliqué 2 Fs to C. Repeat to make a total of 4 appliquéd Cs. Join Cs to Bs as shown in Block Assembly Diagram to make 1 flower block.
 Repeat to make 22 flower blocks.
 2. Referring to Quilt Top Assembly Diagram for placement, join flower blocks, setting squares, side triangles, and corner triangles in diagonal rows. Join rows.
 3. To make top border, join 14 Gs and 13 Hs as shown in Quilt Top Assembly Diagram. (Refer to photograph for color placement.) Repeat to make bottom border.
 To make 1 side border, join 17 Gs and 16 Hs, referring to photograph for color placement. Repeat to make second side border.
 To make 1 corner unit, join 3 Is, referring to photograph for color placement. Repeat to make 4 corner units.
 4. Join borders to edges of quilt top. Join corner units to corners of quilt top, using set-in seams. Refer to Quilt Smart, "Set-in Seams," on page 17.

Quilting
 Quilt Feather Wreath Quilting Pattern in each setting square. Quilt Tea Leaf Quilting Pattern in center of each A and each side triangle. On remainder of quilt, echo-quilt at 1" intervals as shown in photograph.

Finished Edges
 Bind with bias binding made from white.

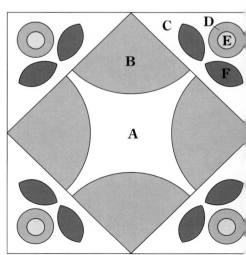

Block Assembly Diagram

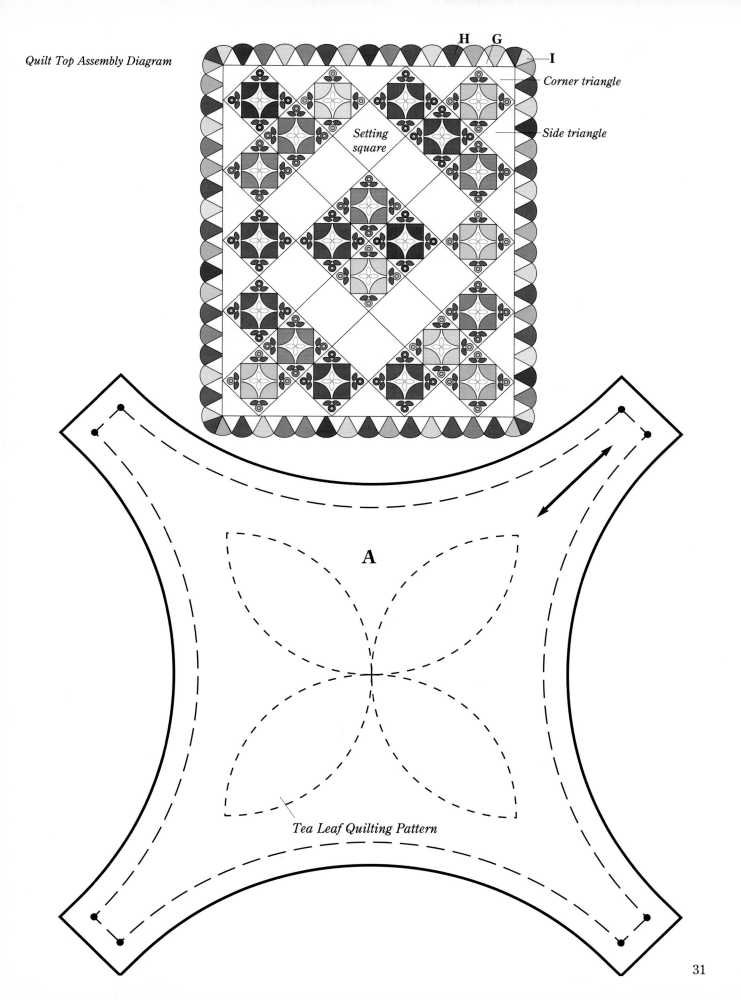

Quilt Top Assembly Diagram

H **G**

I

Corner triangle

Side triangle

Setting square

A

Tea Leaf Quilting Pattern

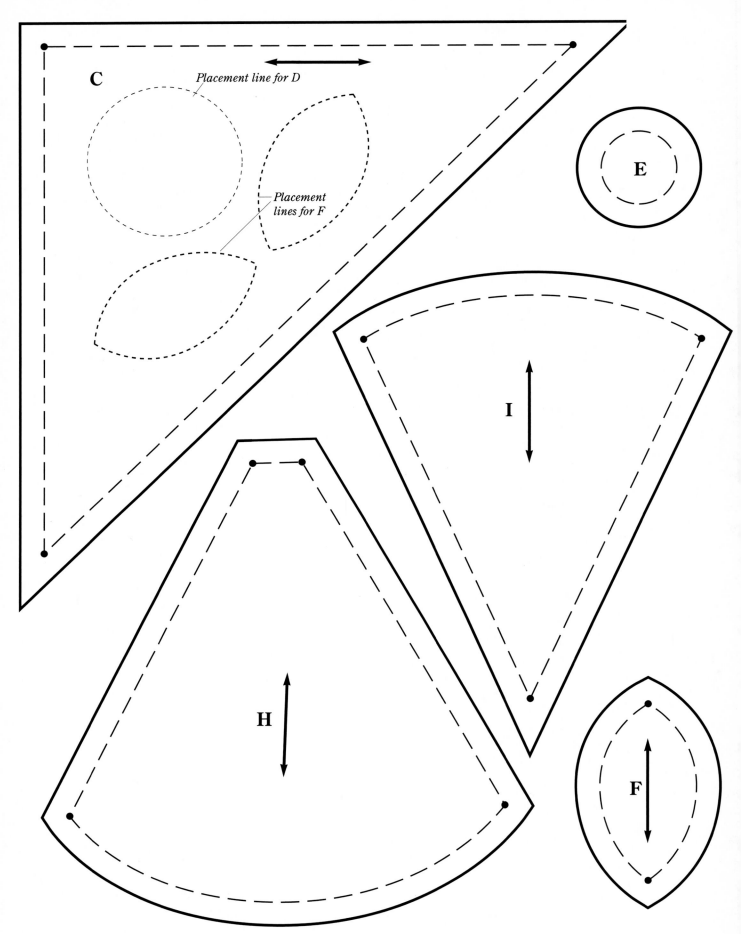

C

Placement line for D

Placement lines for F

E

I

H

F

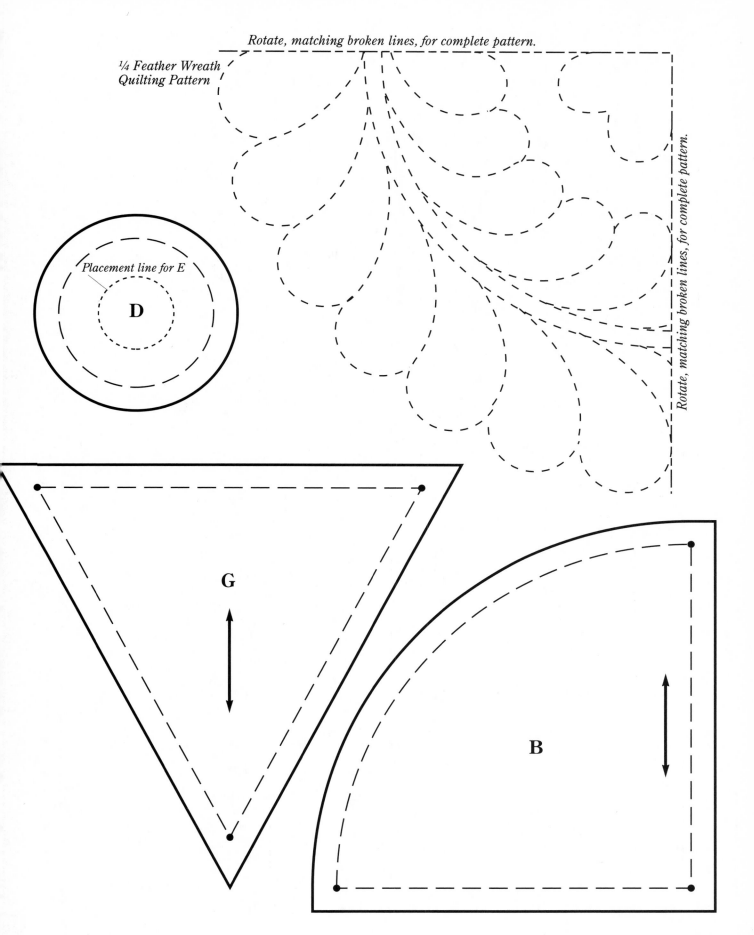

Rotate, matching broken lines, for complete pattern.

¼ Feather Wreath
Quilting Pattern

Rotate, matching broken lines, for complete pattern.

Placement line for E

D

G

B

33

Julie Koch
NILES, MICHIGAN

Julie Koch made her first quilt at age 15 in 4-H club. "My first quilt was a Hawaiian appliqué pattern," Julie says. "My mother helped me cut it out, but I appliquéd the whole top." Succeeding at such a complex first project gave Julie the confidence to continue making quilts that please her, regardless of their level of complexity.

Although most of her work so far has been with traditional patterns, Julie has, during the past year, begun working with original designs and entering her quilts in regional and national shows. "Although I haven't won any of those awards yet," she says, "I hope to change that soon!"

Sunset Serenity
1993

One of the activities many quilters enjoy is swapping charm squares—exchanging print or solid fabric squares of a certain size in order to make scrap quilts using all different fabrics. A charm swap may begin at a guild meeting and grow beyond guild members to include other quilters within the same state. Some collectors advertise in quilting magazines and eventually exchange fabric with pen pals across the United States, as Julie did. "I collected about 1200 charm squares from women all over the U.S. before I started this piece," she says. "The colors remind me of a sunset we saw on a trip to the ocean—all purple and pink."

Sunset Serenity won an award at the 1993 quilt show held by Julie's guild, the Niles Piecemakers. It has also been juried into competitions at the 1994 Mid-Atlantic Quilt Festival in Williamsburg, Virginia, and at the 1994 American Quilter's Society Quilt Show in Paducah, Kentucky.

pieced top across border. Quilt marked lines.

Finished Edges

To make bias binding, cut assorted prints into 2½"-wide bias strips of random lengths. Cut ends of strips on straight grain (at 45° angle to long edge of strip). Join strips along straight grain, varying colors as shown in photograph. Bind edges of quilt.

Block Assembly Diagrams

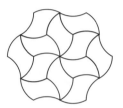

Hexagon Block—Make 22.

Half-Block 1—Make 4.

Half-Block 2—Make 11.

Corner Block 1—Make 1.

Corner Block 2—Make 1.

Sunset Serenity

Finished Quilt Size
70" x 88"

Fabric Requirements

White	2½ yards
Assorted prints	4½ yards or 377 (6") squares
Backing	5½ yards
Assorted prints for bias binding	1 yard

Pieces to Cut
White
  2 (8½" x 70½") border strips
  2 (8½" x 88½") border strips
Assorted prints
  377 pieces

Quilt Top Assembly

1. Following photograph for color placement, arrange pieces on design wall or other large surface. (See Quilt Smart on page 37 for tips on making design wall.) Referring to Block Assembly Diagrams, group pieces into hexagon blocks, half blocks, and corner blocks. Join grouped pieces as shown.

2. Referring to Quilt Top Assembly Diagram, join blocks, half blocks, and corner blocks into vertical rows as shown. Join rows. Trim quilt top as shown in Quilt Top Assembly Diagram.

3. Join 8½" x 70½" white border strips to top and bottom of quilt. Join 8½" x 88½" white border strips to sides of quilt, mitering corners.

4. If desired, cut and appliqué additional pieces onto border as shown in photograph.

Quilting

Quilt each piece ¼" inside seam line. Using template made from pattern piece without seam allowance, mark border, extending pattern from

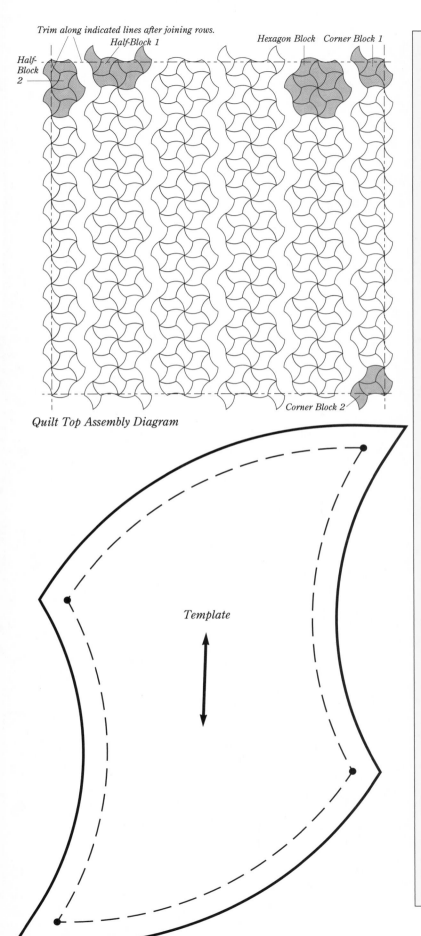

Trim along indicated lines after joining rows.

Half-Block 1

Half-Block 2

Hexagon Block Corner Block 1

Corner Block 2

Quilt Top Assembly Diagram

Template

❖ Quilt Smart

To duplicate the color grouping used in Julie Koch's quilt, you will need to arrange all of the pieces before beginning to sew. Professional quilters often dedicate a wall in their studios for this purpose, paneling it with cork or bulletin board material and then pinning the pieces directly to the wall as the design proceeds. If you don't have the luxury of a dedicated design wall, make a temporary design board to use instead.

- **Flannel sheet:** If you have an empty wall space measuring approximately 6' wide x 7' high that can be temporarily used for layout, the least expensive design board may not be a board at all. Buy approximately 4½ yards of flannel, felt, or polyester fleece (such as Thermolam). Cut it into two lengths of 81" each and stitch them together to make one large sheet measuring about 72" x 81". Pin the sheet to the wall along the top edge. As you place each piece, smooth it against the flannel; the piece will cling to the fuzzy surface. As you decide on the placement of each piece, pin it to the flannel for more security. The sheet can be taken down and rolled up, pins and all, until you are ready to complete the piecing.

- **Free-standing board:** If you don't have enough empty wall space, you will need to construct a free-standing board measuring at least 60" x 72" to accommodate all pieces for the quilt top. If you have room for it, a longer board will be more comfortable to use; you won't be forced to place pieces all the way to the floor. But don't buy a board longer than 92" unless you have high ceilings in your workroom.

Artist's foam-core board, available from art supply and some office supply stores in sheets up to 48" x 96", is an ideal material to use: lightweight and easy to pin. Buy two sheets and trim each to the best length for your space. To hinge the sheets, cut a strip of muslin 4" wide by the length you have chosen. Place the foam-core sheets on the floor, butting long edges. Glue the muslin strip to each sheet, centering the strip over the join line. Let the glue dry and stand the board upright. The hinge allows you to fold it slightly, like a screen, if the board must stand by itself. Or lean it against a wall, desk, or other piece of furniture for a flat surface. If you wish, cover the foam core with flannel, felt, or fleece to enable you to temporarily place your pieces as described above. Or leave the foam core uncovered and pin each piece directly to the board as you place it.

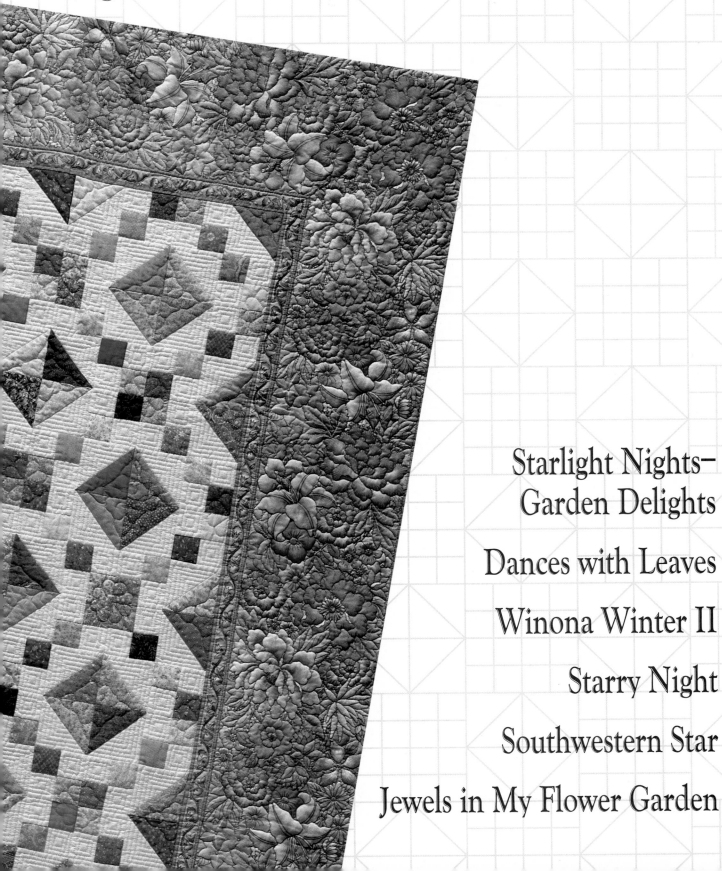

QUILTS ACROSS AMERICA

Starlight Nights–
Garden Delights

Dances with Leaves

Winona Winter II

Starry Night

Southwestern Star

Jewels in My Flower Garden

"How did I start quilting? Well, I bought a book on beginning patchwork because I liked the Christmas project shown— and because it was on sale!"

Judith Hindall
STOW, OHIO

Judith Hindall, an engineering technical specialist for the telephone company, taught herself to quilt three years ago. She had no other quilters in her family as learning resources, so she worked from books and relied upon skills developed in other forms of needlework. She is quick to acknowledge, however, that learning without a teacher has some disadvantages. "I almost always run out of some fabric during a project," Judy says, "and have to figure out some desperate thing to make it work out. But I'm getting better!"

Judy's engineering skills are also put to good use in her quiltmaking. She drafts many of her own patterns, beginning occasionally with traditional blocks and sometimes with original concepts. As with *Starlight Nights–Garden Delights,* the fabric itself sometimes sparks an idea. "I love cats," Judy says, "and I enjoy using cat fabric when I can find it."

Starlight Nights–Garden Delights
1993

The star block Judy used for this quilt is based on Judy Martin's block Scarborough Fair (see "Resources"), redrafted and slightly modified to showcase the cat faces she found hiding among the flowers in the blue-and-pink print fabric. "I chose this fabric because of the cat faces, of course, but also because the colors are beautiful together," Judy says.

"When she was cutting this fabric for me, the lady at the quilt shop told me that she had sold yards and *yards* of this print, and no one had ever before noticed that there were cat faces in it!"

The pieced border is the result of one of those "accidents" Judy has from time to time. "I ran out of the periwinkle blue," she says, "and had

to work out another border treatment. But I think the final border works for the quilt instead of detracting from it."

Starlight Nights–Garden Delights won first place at the 1993 Keep Us in Stitches guild show in Independence, Ohio.

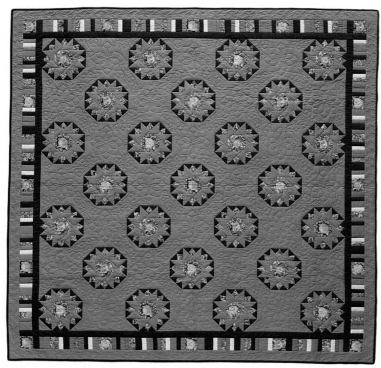

The floral cat fabric Judy used in Starlight Nights–Garden Delights *is a Springs Industries print designed by Marti Michell, and has been discontinued. Look for a similar fabric with floral or other motifs to use in your quilt.*

Starlight Nights – Garden Delights

Finished Quilt Size
84" x 84"

Number of Blocks and Finished Size
25 blocks   10" x 10"

Fabric Requirements
Light blue solid	4½ yards
Pink floral print	1½ to 5 yards*
Navy solid	2½ yards
Green solid	¼ yard
White	¼ yard
Backing	7½ yards
Navy for bias binding	1 yard

*Depends upon repeat of desired motif in print.

Pieces to Cut
Light blue solid
  2 (3" x 79½") outer border strips
  2 (3" x 84½") outer border strips
  24 (10½") setting squares
  300 B
  30 E**
  20 F**
  7 G**

Pink floral print
  4 (3½") corner squares for borders
  25 A†
  200 C
  16 E**
  10 F**
  6 G**
  12 H**
Navy solid
  2 (2½" x 70½") inner border strips
  2 (2½" x 73½") inner border strips
  400 D
  29 E**
  19 F**
  5 G**
Green solid
  27 E**
  9 F**
White
  37 E**

**For pieced border.
†See Quilt Smart on page 44.

Quilt Top Assembly
1. Referring to Block Assembly Diagram, Figure 1, join 1 light blue solid B, 1 pink floral print C, and 2 navy Ds to make 1 pieced triangle. Repeat to make 8 pieced triangles.

Referring to Block Assembly Diagram, Figure 2, join 1 pieced triangle to 1 edge of pink floral print A. Working in a counterclockwise direction, join second pieced triangle to A as shown in Figure 3. Continuing in counterclockwise direction, join 5 more pieced triangles to A. Join last pieced triangle to A using set-in seam, as shown in Figure 4. (See Quilt Smart on page 17 for instructions on stitching set-in seams.)

Referring to Block Assembly Diagram, Figure 5, join 1 light blue solid B to each corner of pieced octagon to complete 1 block. Repeat to make 25 blocks.

2. Referring to Quilt Top Assembly Diagram, join 4 blocks and 3 setting squares to make 1 Row 1. Repeat to make 4 Row 1s.

Join 3 blocks and 4 setting squares to make 1 Row 2. Repeat to make 3 Row 2s.

Join rows alternately as shown.

3. Join 2½" x 70½" navy solid border strips to sides of quilt top. Join 2½" by 73½" navy solid border strips to top and bottom of quilt top, butting corners.

4. Join Es, Fs, Gs, and Hs in random order to make 1 long pieced strip. Cut into 4 (74½"-long) pieced borders. Join 2 pieced borders to sides of quilt. Join 1 (3½") pink floral square to each remaining pieced border. Join to top and bottom of quilt top.

5. Join 3" x 79½" light blue solid border strips to sides of quilt. Join 3" x 84½" light blue solid border strips to top and bottom of quilt, butting corners.

Quilting
Outline-quilt stars. Quilt Rose Quilting Pattern in setting squares. Quilt Rosebud Quilting Pattern diagonally between pieced blocks. Quilt border in-the-ditch.

Finished Edges
Bind with bias binding made from navy.

Block Assembly Diagram

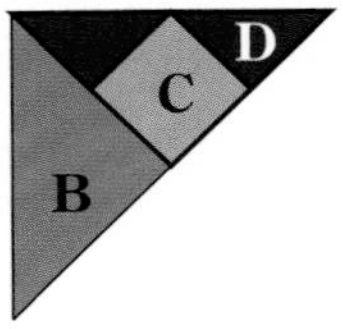

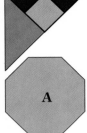

Figure 1

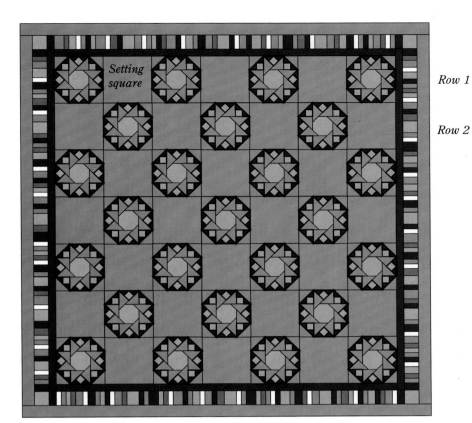

Setting square

Row 1

Row 2

Quilt Top Assembly Diagram

Figure 2

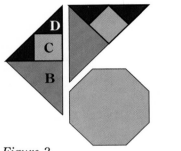

Figure 3

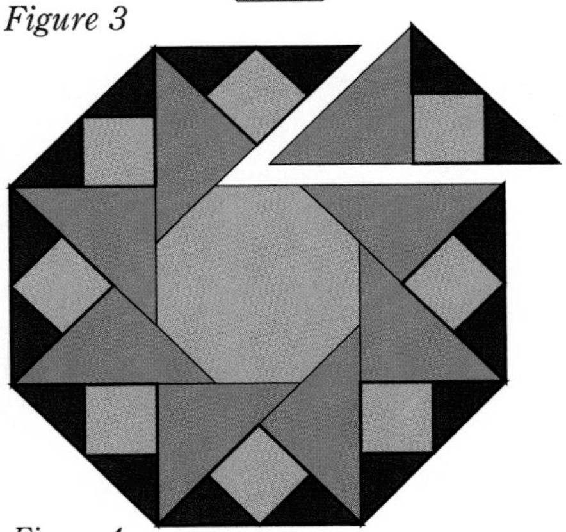

Figure 4

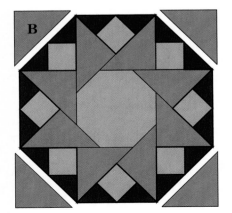

Figure 5

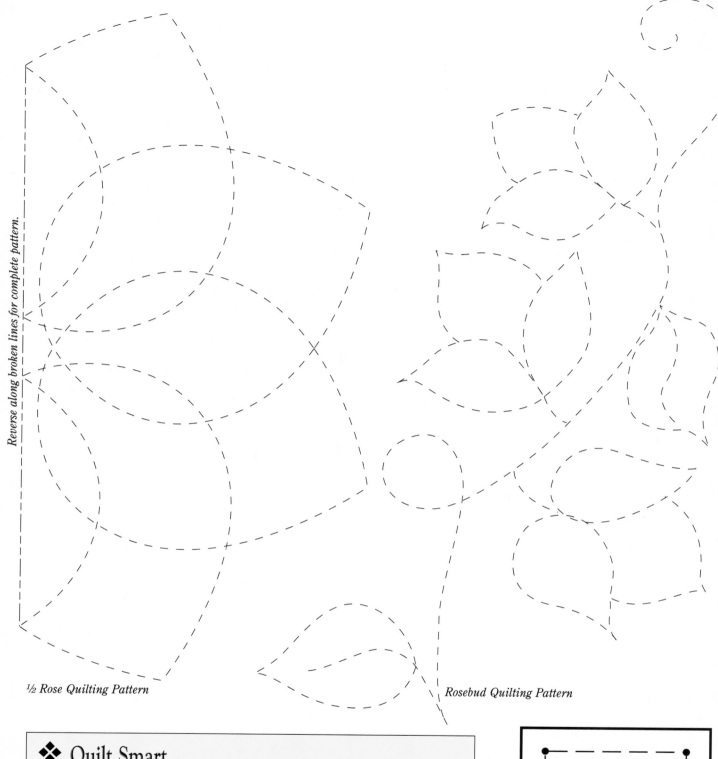

Reverse along broken lines for complete pattern.

½ Rose Quilting Pattern

Rosebud Quilting Pattern

❖ Quilt Smart

Follow these steps to cut As for the center of your stars from the floral print you have chosen.

Using a fine-point permanent marking pen or laundry pen, trace both the sewing and cutting lines for pattern piece A onto a sheet of plastic template material. Cut out along both sets of lines to create a window template. (Use a craft knife to cut along the inside line.) Place the window on the right side of your fabric, moving it until the framed motif pleases you. Holding the template in place, trace around the outside cutting line for a perfect ¼" seam allowance around the chosen motif.

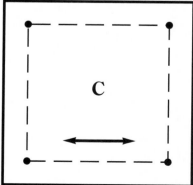

C

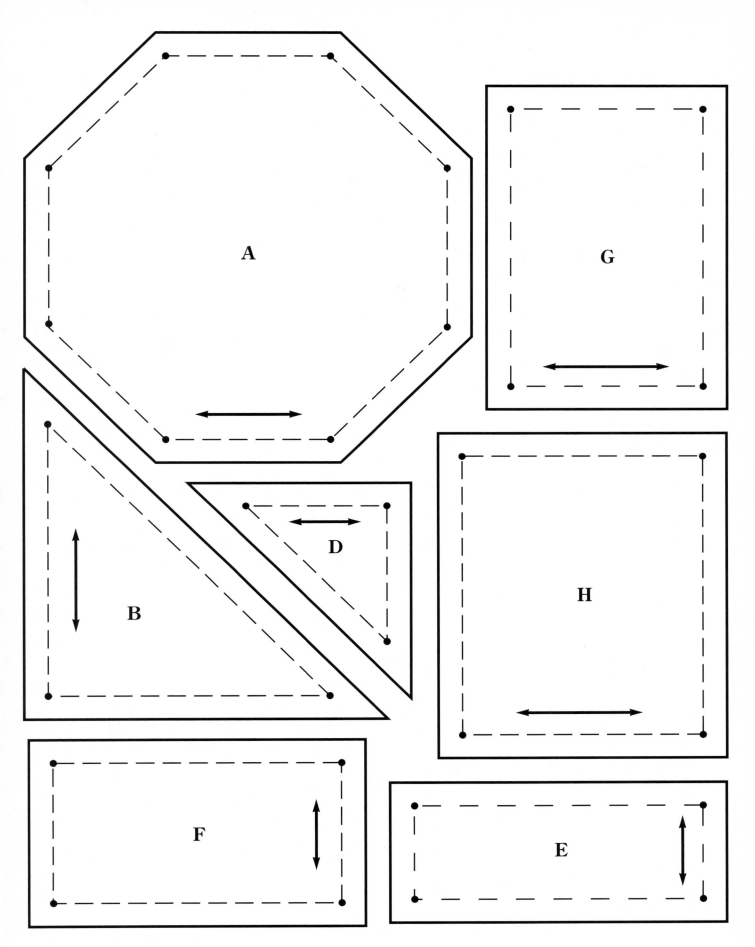

"Although my work looks very traditional, I like putting together really different-looking pieces."

Judith Sandstrom
FT. WASHINGTON, PENNSYLVANIA

In the 15 years since she took her first quilting class at a local fabric store, Judith Sandstrom has continually pushed herself to learn and grow as a quilt-maker. "Through taking classes and trying new techniques, I found that my greatest pleasure came from designing my own quilts," Judith says. "Although my work looks very traditional—geometric, balanced, and subtle—I like putting together really different-looking pieces."

In 1989, Judith began selling her original designs to quilt magazines and currently has about six articles appearing each year. "I also enjoy making special commemorative and commissioned pieces for family and friends," she says. "Now that my four children have grown older, I have much more time for quilting."

Dances with Leaves
1994

Judith's original design for *Dances with Leaves* was sparked by the colors of the leaf print fabric that reminded her of the colors of autumn. "I wanted to make a pieced quilt," she says, "but one that would give the illusion of motion in the windblown, swirling leaves." The pinwheel star she used to represent the leaves conveys the feeling of movement. The interlocking pieced border gives the impression of leaves lying on the ground in piles, raked off the beige sidewalk neatly lined with plants.

Dances with Leaves

Finished Quilt Size
46" x 46"

Fabric Requirements
Beige	1¼ yards
Dark green stripe	1⅓ yards
Red/green stripe	1 yard
Leaf print	¾ yard
Light green floral	⅛ yard
Dark green floral	⅛ yard
Gold print	⅛ yard
Red solid	⅛ yard
Light red print	⅛ yard
Medium red print	⅛ yard
Dark red print	⅛ yard
Backing	3 yards
Medium red print for bias binding	¾ yard

Pieces to Cut
Beige
    4 (4" x 35") border strips
    2 (8⅜") squares*
    16 A
    72 B
    4 C
    1 D
    4 E
Dark green stripe
    4 (1½" x 46") outer border strips
    8 (1½" x 35") inner border strips
Red/green stripe
    4 (1¾" x 35") inner border strips
Leaf print
    112 A
    112 B
Light green floral
    10 A
    40 B
Dark green floral
    10 A
    40 B
Gold print
    10 A
    40 B
Red solid
    10 A
    40 B
Light red print
    10 A
    40 B
Medium red print
    4 A
    16 B
Dark red print
    10 A
    40 B
*Cut each square in half diagonally to make 4 corner triangles.

Quilt Top Assembly
1. To make medallion, join 16 beige As, 8 leaf print As, 2 light green floral As, 2 dark green floral As, 2 gold As, 2 light red print As, 2 medium red print As, 2 dark red print As, 72 beige Bs, 8 leaf print Bs, 8 light green floral Bs, 8 dark green floral Bs, 8 gold Bs, 8 light red print Bs, 8 medium red print Bs, 8 dark red print Bs, 4 beige Cs, 1 beige D, and 4 beige Es as shown in Medallion Assembly Diagram. Join beige corner triangles to corners to complete medallion.

2. To make 1 inner border, join 1 (1¾" x 35") red/green stripe border strip, 1 (1½" x 35") dark green stripe border strip, 1 (4" x 35") beige border strip, and 1 (1½" x 35") dark green

stripe border strip. Repeat to make 4 inner borders. Join to sides of medallion, mitering corners.

3. To make star border, refer to photograph for color placement and join 2 As and 2 Bs to make 1 Unit 1, as shown in Pieced Border Unit Assembly Diagram. Repeat to make 52 Units 1s. In same manner, join 1 A and 4 Bs to make 1 Unit 2. Repeat to make 52 Unit 2s. Referring to Quilt Top Assembly Diagram and photograph for color placement, join 11 Unit 1s and 12 Unit 2s to make top border; repeat for bottom border. Join to top and bottom of quilt. In same manner, join 15 Unit 1s and 14 Unit 2s to make 1 side border; repeat to make second side border. Join to sides of quilt, butting corners.

4. Join 1½" x 46" dark green stripe border strips to sides of quilt, mitering corners.

Quilting
Quilt in-the-ditch around stars and green stripe borders. Quilt border, medallion, and corner triangles as desired.

Finished Edges
Bind with bias binding made from medium red print fabric.

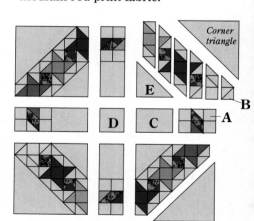

Medallion Assembly Diagram

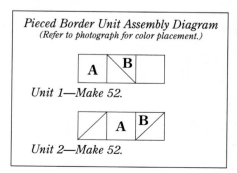

Pieced Border Unit Assembly Diagram
(Refer to photograph for color placement.)

Unit 1—Make 52.

Unit 2—Make 52.

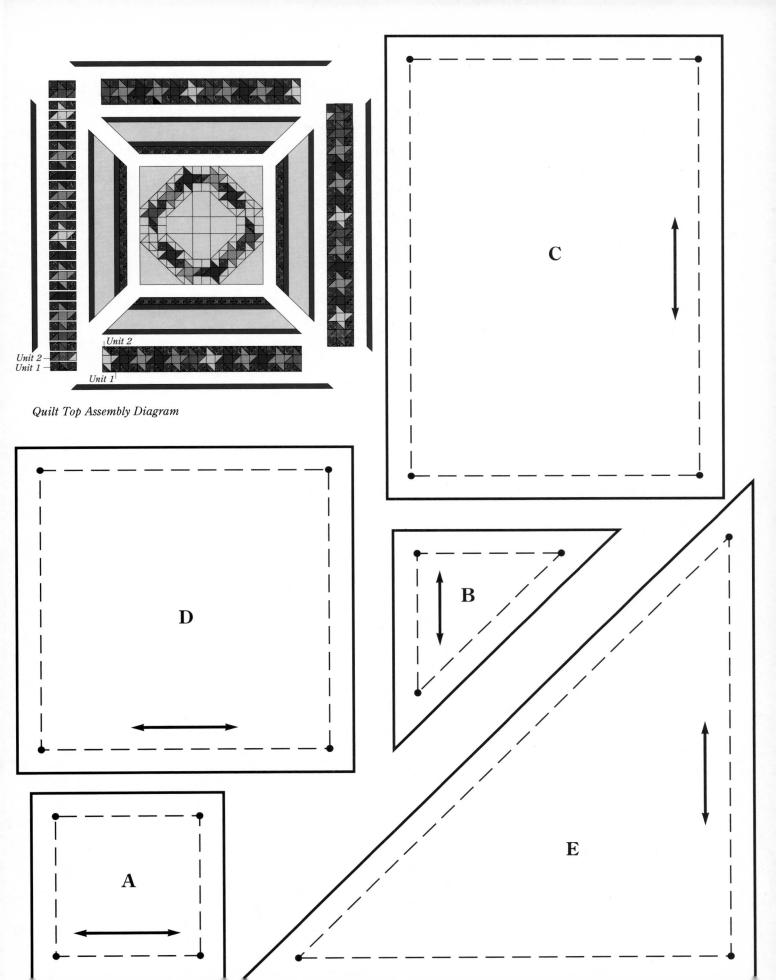

Quilt Top Assembly Diagram

Unit 2
Unit 1

Unit 2
Unit 1

C

D

B

A

E

"Quilting has given me a vehicle to express my love of nature and feelings of optimism about the future."

Ann Fahl
RACINE, WISCONSIN

Ann Fahl tried many forms of needle arts before finding her way to quilting. She began sewing at 12, went on to study textiles and clothing in college, and worked with embroidery, weaving, and machine appliqué along the way. But it wasn't until she signed up for a quilting class 15 years ago that she found her creative medium. "Quilting enables me to work with things I love: color, fabric, and stitchery," Ann says.

Ann's quilts have won numerous awards and have been exhibited both in national quilt shows and in art shows such as the recent "Contemporary Quilts: Four Visions in Fiber" at the Stocker Center Gallery in Elyria, Ohio. And Neiman Marcus, the department store chain based in Dallas, recently bought several of her quilts to display as permanent artwork in their new stores.

Winona Winter II
1993

Winona Winter II, as its name suggests, is the second wintry leaf quilt Ann has made. Her first *Winona Winter* sold so quickly that she never had time to enter it into a quilt show. "So I decided to make this second piece similar to the first one but expanded the background colors from just blue to reds, violets, and blues," Ann explains.

The leaf patterns used for *Winona Winter II* were taken from real leaves Ann picked from trees at her cottage on Winona Lake, Indiana. "The simple theme of triangles, illusion veiling, and snowy white leaves was meant to get my creativity recharged at the end of a long Wisconsin winter," Ann says.

Ann has embellished Winona Winter II *with layered tulle (also called "bridal illusion" and available in the bridal department of fabric stores) to recall wintry skies. She has also heavily machine-quilted the background using contrasting thread and added beads in places "to add the sparkle of ice to the quilt," she says.*

Winona Winter II

Finished Quilt Size
60" x 37½"

Fabric Requirements
Assorted dark red prints 1¼ yards
Assorted medium
  red prints   2½ yards
Assorted blue prints   1¼ yards
Assorted purple prints ⅔ yard
Lavender print   ¼ yard
White solid   ½ yard
Blue/white stripe   ½ yard
Navy solid   ¼ yard
White tulle (optional)   ¼ yard
Backing   2½ yards
Lavender print
  for bias binding   ½ yard

Pieces to Cut
Assorted dark red prints
  72 A
Assorted medium red prints
  148 A
Assorted blue prints
  62 A
Assorted purple prints
  38 A
Lavender print
  6 B
White solid
  7 C
  2 D
  23 F

Blue/white stripe
  1 C
  7 D
  9 E
  4 F
Navy solid
  11 E

Quilt Top Assembly
1. Following Quilt Top Assembly Diagram and referring to photograph for color placement, join 32 As in pairs to make 16 squares as shown. Join squares to make 1 row. Repeat, referring to photograph for color placement, to make 10 rows. Join rows.

2. If desired, cut edges of white tulle in random curves to suggest a snowy effect. Place tulle on quilt top; straightstitch edges to secure. (Because tulle does not ravel, edges need not be turned under or otherwise finished.)

3. Referring to photograph for guidance, arrange Bs, Cs, Ds, Es, and Fs in pleasing arrangement across quilt top. Pin pieces in place. Appliqué each piece to quilt top.

Quilting
Outline-quilt around each appliquéd leaf. Quilt remainder in-the-ditch, or quilt as desired.

Finished Edges
Bind with bias binding made from lavender print fabric.

Quilt Top Assembly Diagram

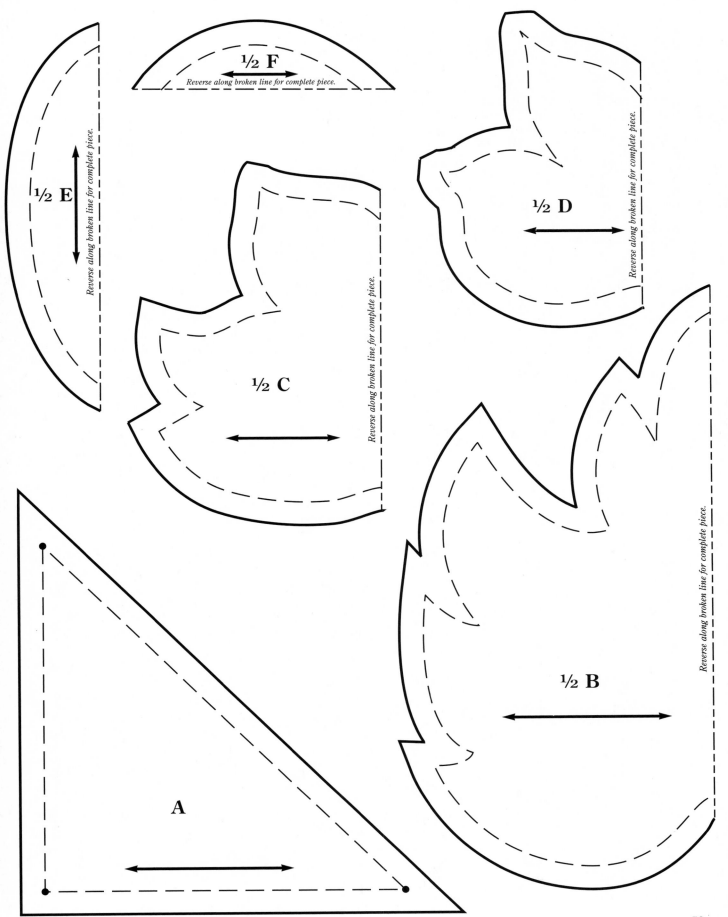

½ F
Reverse along broken line for complete piece.

½ E
Reverse along broken line for complete piece.

½ D
Reverse along broken line for complete piece.

½ C
Reverse along broken line for complete piece.

½ B
Reverse along broken line for complete piece.

A

"Quilting is my way of holding hands with the past."

Ethel Taylor Jordan
CORYDON, IOWA

"Start with the traditional, and then follow the dream!" Ask Ethel Jordan where she gets her ideas for quilts, and that's what she'll tell you.

Ethel has been making quilts since she was very young. "I sat under the frame as my mother quilted," she says, "and watched her hands as she sewed. I really can't remember a time when I couldn't use a needle." She shares her skills with others by teaching beginning quilting classes for women in her area and by chairing local quilt shows. "Quilting is my way of holding hands with the past," she says. "Making a quilt is a treasure from the past reinvested in the future."

Starry Night
1988

"I saw a quilt made from this pattern when I visited a friend in Pennsylvania," Ethel says, "and I knew I had to have one like it." Ethel's friend supplied a copy of the article in *Needlecraft Today,* which contained the patterns and instructions for this old quilt block; the article also mentioned that the pattern was developed in Germany and had been brought to the United States many years before. Ethel chose colors reminiscent of the night sky,

reflecting the feelings of space and beauty that the quilt pattern gave her. Although she quilts professionally as well as making many quilts for family and friends, *Starry Night* is one quilt Ethel intends to keep.

"This quilt reminds me of my childhood in the 1930s," Ethel says, "and the summer nights of sleeping on the floor in front of the doorway to catch the breeze. Some nights, we would sleep out in the open, where the stars were our only night lights."

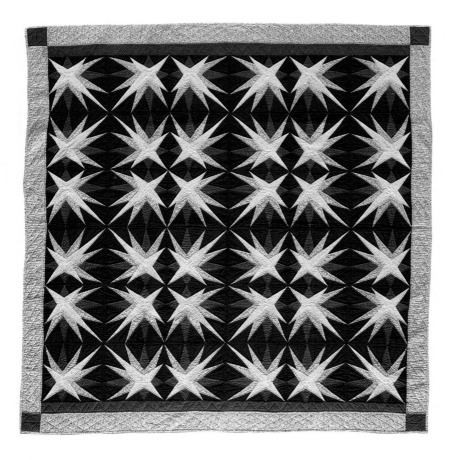

Dark blue print
   2 (2½" x 72½") border strips
   4 (4½") corner squares
   72 C
   72 C rev.
   72 G
   72 G rev.
Navy solid
   72 D
   72 D rev.
   36 F
   36 F rev.
   72 H
   72 H rev.
   36 J
   36 J rev.

Quilt Top Assembly

1. Referring to Block Assembly Diagram, join 3 white As, 1 white B, 2 dark blue print Cs, 2 dark blue print Cs rev., 2 navy solid Ds, 2 navy solid Ds rev., 1 light blue print E, 1 light blue print E rev., 1 navy solid F, 1 navy solid F rev., 2 dark blue print Gs, 2 dark blue print Gs rev., 2 navy solid Hs, 2 navy solid Hs rev., 1 light blue print I, 1 light blue print I rev., 1 navy solid J, 1 navy solid J rev. to make 1 block. Repeat to make 36 blocks.

Starry Night

Finished Quilt Size
80" x 84"

Number of Blocks and Finished Size

36 blocks	12" x 12"

Fabric Requirements

White	2½ yards
Light blue print	3½ yards
Dark blue print	2¼ yards
Navy solid	6 yards
Backing	5¼ yards
Light blue print for bias binding	1 yard

Pieces to Cut
White
   108 A
   36 B
Light blue print
   2 (4½" x 76½") border strips
   2 (4½" x 72½") border strips
   36 E
   36 E rev.
   36 I
   36 I rev.

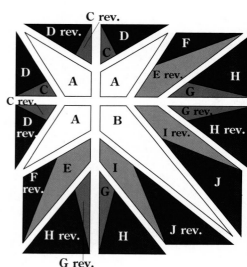

Block Assembly Diagram

2. Referring to Quilt Top Assembly Diagram for block orientation, join blocks in 6 rows of 6 blocks each. Join rows.

3. Join 2½" x 72½" dark blue print border strips to top and bottom of quilt. Join 4½" x 72½" light blue print border strips to top and bottom of quilt.

To make 1 side border, join 1 (4½")
dark blue print square to each end
of 1 (4½" x 76½") light blue print
border strip. Repeat for second side
border. Join to sides of quilt, butting
corners.

Quilting
   Outline-quilt all block pieces. Quilt
borders as desired.

Finished Edges
   Bind with bias binding made from
light blue print fabric.

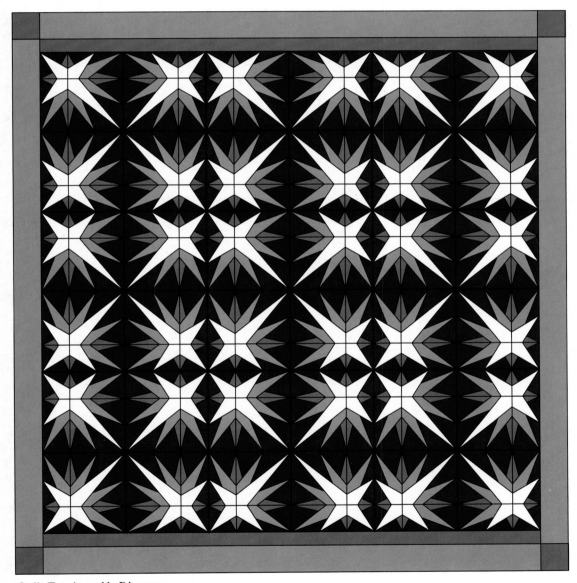

Quilt Top Assembly Diagram

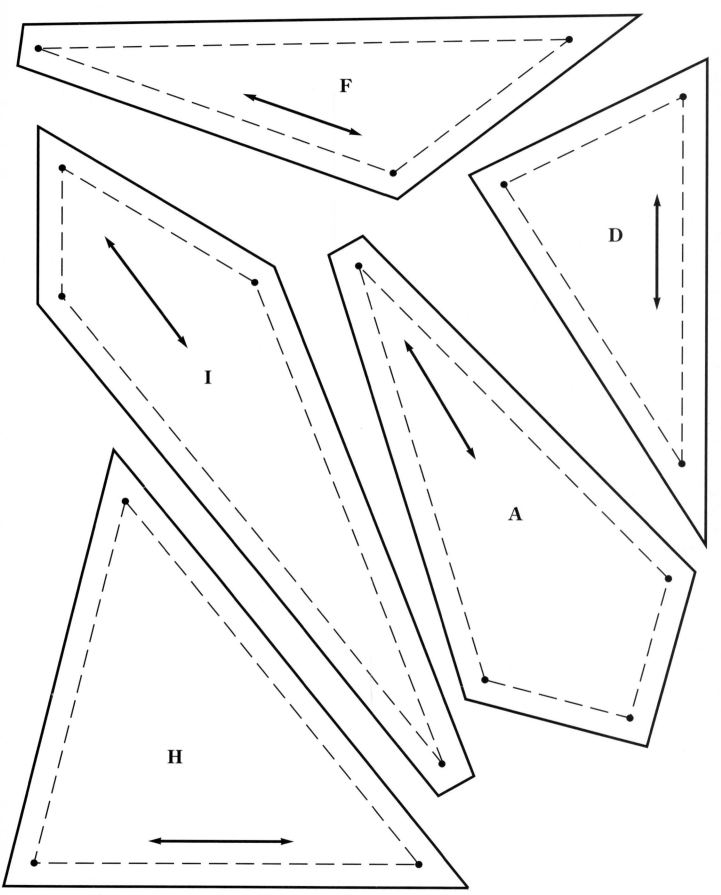

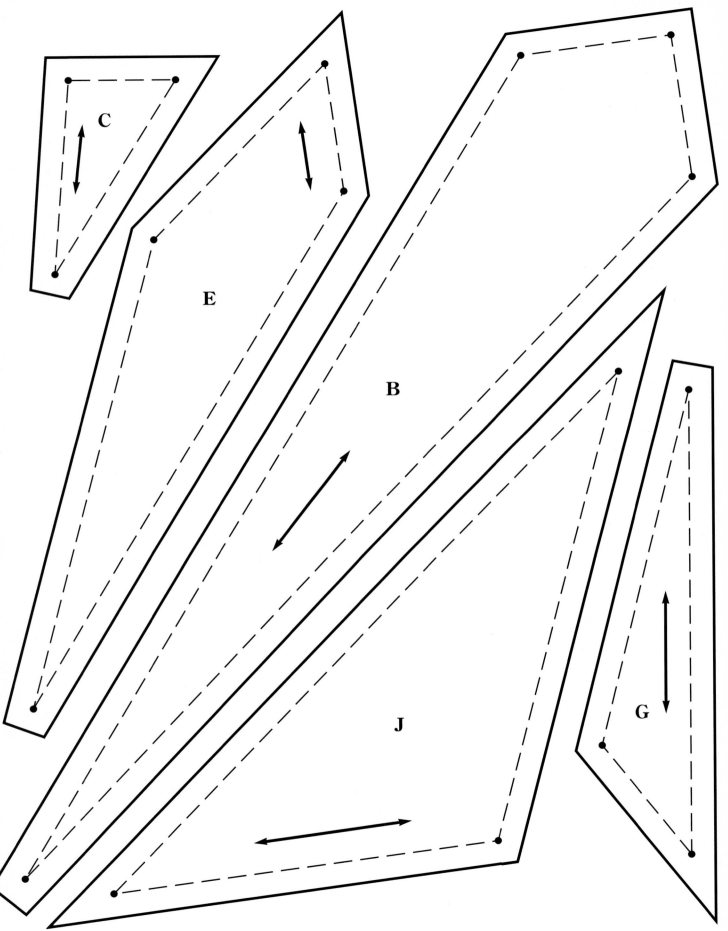

C

E

B

J

G

*"I've learned never to say 'never.'
I started as a screen printer and
my next project will be a full-sized
appliquéd quilt!"*

Fern Stewart
DES MOINES, IOWA

"**M**y kids tell their friends they live in a padded house," Fern Stewart says with a smile. "Quilts are on the walls, draped over furniture, and of course, on all the beds!"

A mother of three school-age children and full-time employee of the Parks and Recreation Board, Fern has learned to make every quilting moment count. "I'll 'machine' anything!" she says. "Piecing, quilting, even appliqué. My free time is limited and machine work—done well—is very acceptable."

She passes that "can do" philosophy to her quilting students as well. "One of my most popular classes is a couples' class I teach every Valentine's Day," she says. "Working together, a couple can finish a full-size quilt top during the 6-hour class. Usually the guys rotary-cut the pieces and the women sew, but some of my repeat students are branching out. I tell the men they *can* learn to use the sewing machine. Go for it!"

Southwestern Star
1990

Southwestern Star had its beginnings in a "mystery quilt" class Fern took from Liz Porter in 1989. In a mystery class, the students bring specified supplies and fabric without knowing what the quilt project will be. They cut and stitch following the teacher's instructions, watching the mystery unfold as the quilt tops are assembled.

"Liz specified three contrasting colors," Fern says, "so I brought fabric in black, white, and electric blue. To say it was striking was an understatement!"

Fern loved her finished mystery quilt and soon planned to make a second one. "I knew I wanted to expand on the original and put something of my own spin on it,"

she says. Experimenting with a run of colors in the Southwestern palette she loves, Fern arranged pieces on a flannel design wall until she was satisfied.

"I started this quilt on a Friday and had it pieced the following Monday," she says. "I tend to become possessed when I tackle a design I love."

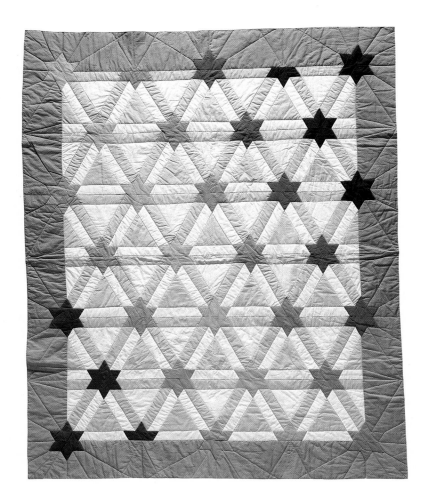

Pieces to Cut
Brown
  2 (8" x 84½") border strips
  2 (8" x 68½") border strips
Off-white
  21 A
  69 B
  3 D
  3 D rev.
  3 E
  3 E rev.
Beige
  21 A
  69 B
  3 D
  3 D rev.
  3 E
  3 E rev.
Light purple
  39 C
Medium purple
  30 C
Dark purple
  21 C
Peach
  39 C
Pink
  30 C
Dark red
  21 C

Quilt Top Assembly
  1. Referring to Block 1 Assembly Diagram, join 1 off-white A, 3 beige Bs, and 3 Cs (referring to photograph for color placement) to make 1 Block 1. Repeat to make 21 Block 1s. In same manner, make 21 Block 2s, 3 Right Half-Block 1s, 3 Left Half-Block 1s, 3 Right Half-Block 2s, and 3 Left Half-Block 2s.
  2. Join remaining Cs in groups as shown in Quilt Top Assembly Diagram. Set aside.

Southwestern Star

Finished Quilt Size
68" x 84"

**Number of Blocks and
Finished Size**
42 blocks   11½" x 13¼"

Fabric Requirements
Brown	2½ yards
Off-white	1¾ yards
Beige	1¾ yards
Light purple	¼ yard
Medium purple	¼ yard
Dark purple	¼ yard
Peach	¼ yard
Pink	¼ yard
Dark red	¼ yard
Backing	5¼ yards
Off-white fabric for bias binding	1 yard

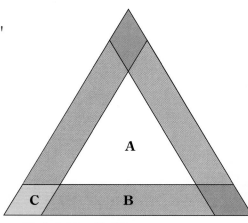

Block 1 Assembly Diagram

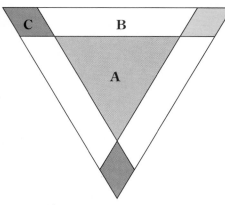

Block 2 Assembly Diagram

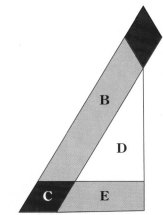

Right Half-Block Assembly Diagram

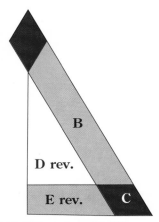

Left Half-Block Assembly Diagram

Quilting
Quilt each block piece in-the-ditch. Quilt border in radiating lines, following seams in appliquéd stars, or quilt as desired.

Finished Edges
Bind with bias binding made from off-white fabric.

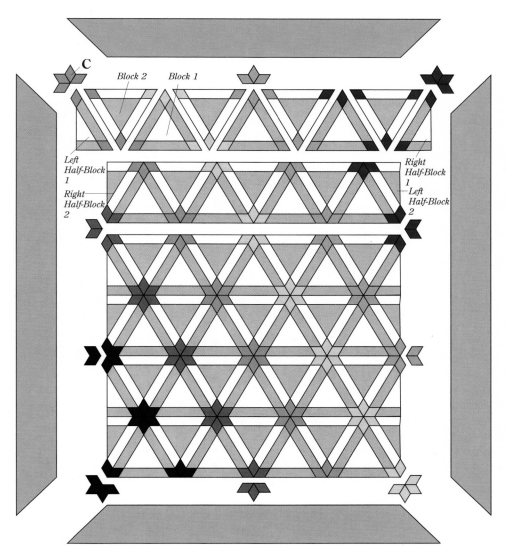

Quilt Top Assembly Diagram

3. Following Quilt Top Assembly Diagram and referring to photograph for color placement, join blocks and half-blocks in rows. Join rows.

4. Join 8" x 68½" brown border strips to top and bottom of quilt. Join 8" x 84½" brown border strips to sides of quilt, mitering corners.

5. Referring to photograph for color placement, appliqué remaining Cs to border as shown in Quilt Top Assembly Diagram.

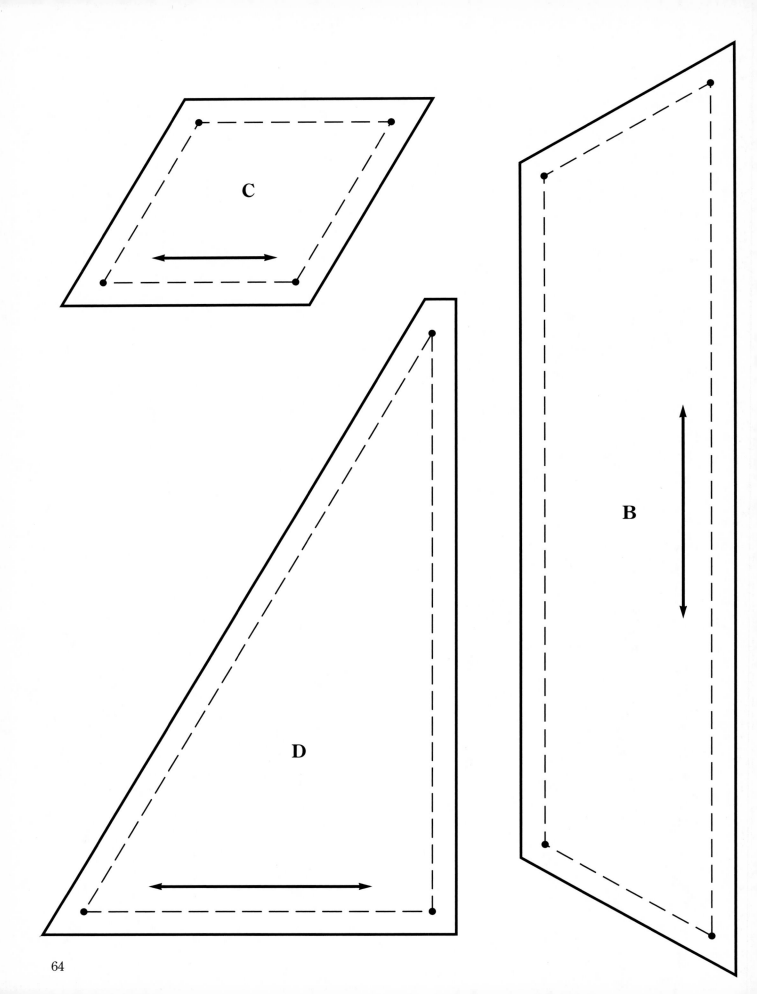

C

B

D

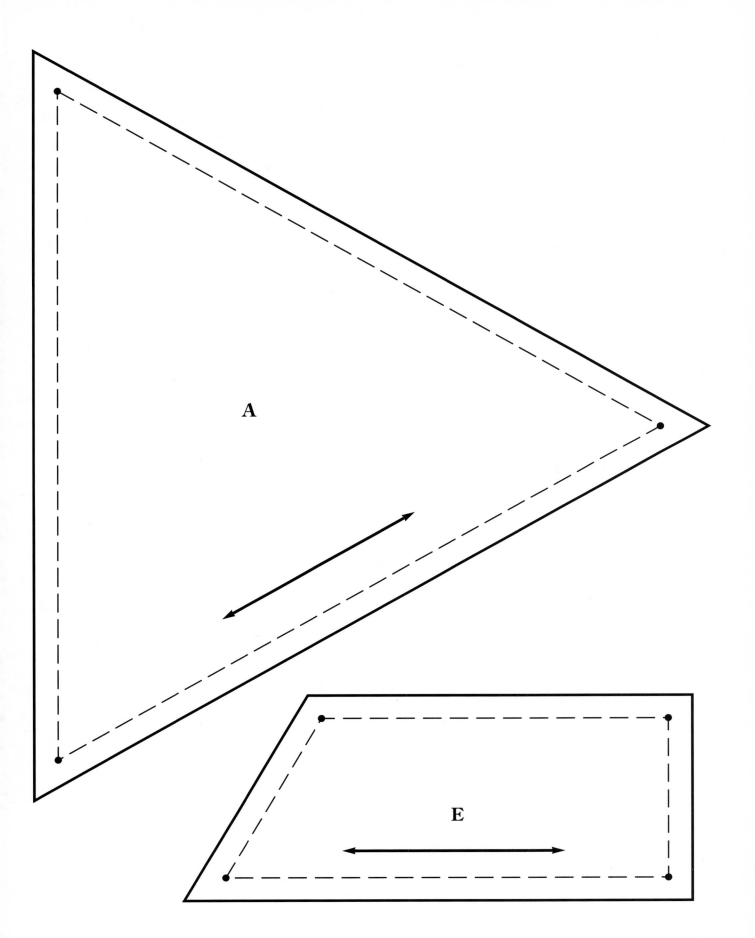

A

E

Elgenia B. Sumner
BIRMINGHAM, ALABAMA

Ask Jean Sumner for the secret to her prize-winning quilt designs, and she answers simply, "Wallpaper books and flower gardens!" But her exquisite quilting skills, color sense, and spirit of adventure also play a large part in the beautiful results. "I enjoy a large variety of quilting techniques," Jean says. "I tend to get bored very easily doing just one thing over and over." She also searches for unusual fabrics to use in her quilts, buying from decorator fabric stores to get the florals she prefers.

"The creativity that quilting offers is very challenging to me," Jean says. "I have so many ideas for quilts, I know I'll never make them all."

Jewels in My Flower Garden
1994

After taking a quilting class on the traditional Jewel Box pattern, Jean began to play with the possibilities of the design. "Each year, the Museum of the American Quilter's Society holds a contest on new interpretations of traditional patterns," Jean says. "Jewel Box was not on their list, but the contest gave me the idea to do my own version of this pattern."

The stunning floral border, meticulous quilting, and mock corded binding are the finishing touches that give *Jewels in My Flower Garden* its special appeal. Although it has been exhibited at only two shows since its completion, the quilt has won two Viewers' Choice ribbons, a Judge's Choice, and a first place ribbon for large pieced quilts.

Quilt Top Assembly

1. Following Block Assembly Diagram, join 16 white As, 16 assorted print As, 8 white Bs, and 8 assorted print Bs to make 1 block. Repeat to make 30 blocks.

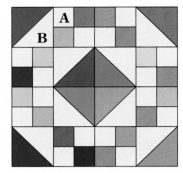

Block Assembly Diagram

2. Join blocks in 6 rows of 5 blocks each. Join rows.

3. To make top border, join 1 (1¾" x 82") aqua stripe border to each long edge of 1 (8¾" x 82") aqua floral border. Repeat to make bottom border. Join to top and bottom of quilt. In same manner, make side borders. Join to sides of quilt, mitering corners.

Quilting

Quilt all pieces in-the-ditch. Echo-quilt white As and Bs at ¼"-intervals. Quilt floral border following flower motifs in print. Or quilt as desired.

Finished Edges

To make "corded" binding, trim backing fabric even with edges of quilt top but *do not trim* excess batting. Following instructions in steps 1-6 of "Making Binding" on page 143, make bias binding from aqua solid; press under ¼" on 1 long edge of binding strip. Attach raw edge of binding to quilt, referring to instructions in "Attaching Binding" on page 143.

Working from back side of quilt and beginning at midpoint of 1 side, tightly roll excess batting to form "cord." Whipstitch batting cord to baste roll in place. Fold binding over cord, aligning folded edge of binding with seam at edge of quilt. Blindstitch or whipstitch binding to backing.

Or if desired, bind edge with bias binding made from aqua solid, following instructions on page 143.

Jewels in My Flower Garden

Finished Quilt Size
81½" x 93½"

Number of Blocks and Finished Size
30 blocks	12" x 12"

Fabric Requirements
Aqua stripe	2¾ yards
Aqua floral	2¾ yards
White	2¾ yards
Assorted prints	2¾ yards
Backing	5¾ yards
Aqua solid for bias binding	1 yard

Pieces to Cut
Aqua stripe
    4 (1¾" x 94") border strips
    4 (1¾" x 82") border strips
Aqua floral
    2 (8¾" x 94") border strips
    2 (8¾" x 82") border strips
White
    480 A
    240 B
Assorted prints
    480 A
    240 B

Quilt Top Assembly Diagram

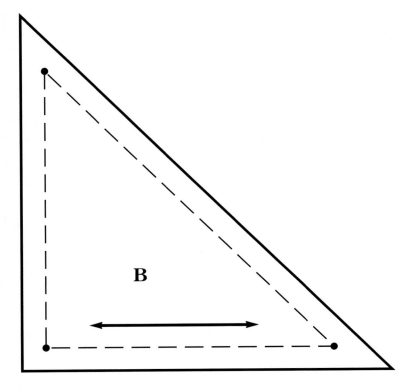

B

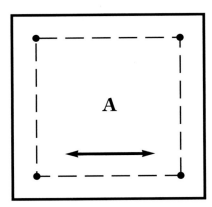

A

TRADITIONS IN QUILTING

"I love choosing colors and piecing squares. I wish I could keep a quilt up on a frame all the time."

Corrie Corkern
FRANKLINTON, LOUISIANA

Corrie Corkern, an accomplished seamstress, began quiltmaking early in her married life with the purchase of a quilt kit featuring appliquéd red poppies. By the time her first child was born a year later, she had completed only about one-fourth of the appliqué. "Over the next 20 years or so," Corrie says, "I was so busy raising my children that I never got around to finishing the red poppy quilt." It wasn't until the mid-1960s that she finished the quilt, entered it in the Washington Parish Fair, and won a blue ribbon. "I couldn't wait to start another one!" Corrie says. "From then on, I seldom missed entering a quilt at the Fair, and so far each quilt I have entered has won a blue ribbon."

For many years, Corrie also enjoyed sewing for her daughters and granddaughters. From the accumulated scraps, she now makes clothing for the porcelain dolls she crafts, as well as creating new quilts for family and friends.

Arkansas Crossroads
1993

Looking for a pattern that would use some of her fabric scraps, Corrie found the Arkansas Crossroads block in a book of scrap quilt patterns and knew immediately that it was the one she wanted to make. "I especially liked the 'crossroad' it made," she says, "and I knew that my grandson Jeff, an architect, would like the lines created by the pattern and the bright colors." Using as many different scraps as possible, Corrie finished the quilt during the summer of 1993. *Arkansas Crossroads* won a blue ribbon at the 1993 Washington Parish Fair.

Assorted light prints
  320 A
  320 B
Assorted medium prints
  320 A
  320 B
Assorted dark prints
  320 A

Quilt Top Assembly

1. Following Block Assembly Diagram and referring to photograph for color placement, join 4 light print As, 4 medium print As, 4 dark print As, 4 light print Bs, and 4 medium print Bs to make 1 block. Repeat to make 80 blocks.

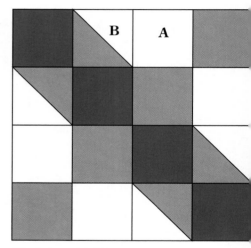

Block Assembly Diagram

Although the finished quilt looks extremely complicated, Arkansas Crossroads *is very easy to piece. Notice how Corrie has arranged the red scraps in her central blocks to form a diamond-shaped medallion.*

Experiment with color placement as you put your quilt together. You may wish to make a design wall (see Quilt Smart *on page 37) to help you arrange your blocks.*

Arkansas Crossroads

Finished Quilt Size
80" x 96"

Number of Blocks and Finished Size
80 blocks   8" x 8"

Fabric Requirements
Red print	2½ yards
Yellow print	2⅜ yards
Assorted light prints	3 yards
Assorted medium prints	3 yards
Assorted dark prints	2 yards
Backing	5¾ yards
Red print for bias binding	1 yard

Pieces to Cut
Red print
  2 (6½" x 80½") outer border strips
  2 (6½" x 84½") outer border strips
Yellow print
  2 (2½" x 68½") inner border strips
  2 (2½" x 80½") inner border strips

2. Following Quilt Top Assembly Diagram and turning blocks to alternate diagonal stripes as shown, join 8 blocks to make 1 row. Repeat to make 10 rows. Join rows.

3. Join 2½" x 80½" yellow print borders to sides of quilt. Join 2½" x 68½" yellow print borders to top and bottom of quilt, butting corners.

4. Join 6½" x 84½" red print borders to sides of quilt. Join 6½" x 80½" red print borders to top and bottom of quilt, butting corners.

Quilting
Quilt in-the-ditch around each star and around each group of 4 squares; or quilt as desired.

Finished Edges
Bind with bias binding made from red print.

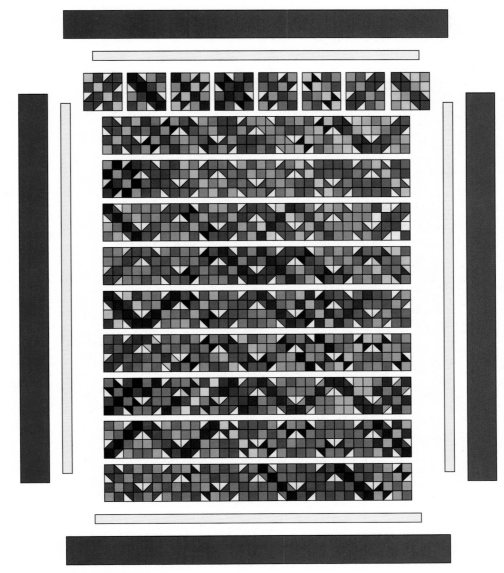

Quilt Top Assembly Diagram

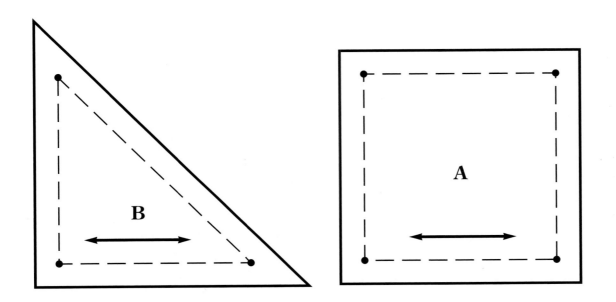

Lila Taylor Scott
MARIETTA, GEORGIA

Lila Taylor Scott never knew that her mother quilted until she found two sets of completed quilt blocks after her mother's death. "My daughter asked me to complete one of the quilts because it was a part of her grandmother," Lila says. "I went to the library and got all the books they had on quilting. I went to a store that had a quilt frame set up and asked them for help. Then I bought some needles and went home to begin."

Since that time, Lila has become immersed in quilting. She has finished more than 30 pieces, including seven bed quilts. In 1988, on the advice of a friend, she joined East Cobb Quilter's Guild. "It's simply changed my life. My closest friends are members of my guild," she says. "We meet once a week in each other's homes, each working on her own project. Through the guild I have taken classes, been able to show my quilts, and made lots of friends. Quilters need praise and encouragement—and the guild gives us both."

Stormy Night
1993

Stormy Night is the result of a monthly block contest among the members of East Cobb Quilter's Guild. Twenty-one members, including Lila, made blocks from the traditional Storm at Sea pattern in blue, purple, and green. The names of each quilter who had made a block were entered into a drawing, and Lila won, taking the blocks home with her. To finish the top, she pieced nine more blocks and designed the pieced border to showcase the purple print, one of her favorite fabrics.

"This is my favorite of all the quilts I have made, and I have it on my bed," Lila says. "The blocks seemed to jump into position as I made it, and I really love the deep jewel-tone colors."

Stormy Night has been shown at the 1993 East Cobb Quilter's Guild show.

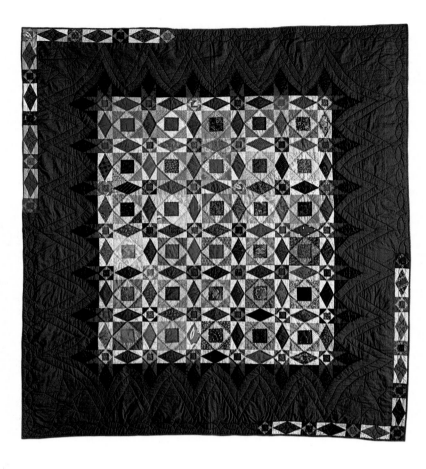

Stormy Night

Finished Quilt Size
78" x 87"

**Number of Blocks and
Finished Size**
30 blocks   6" x 6"

Fabric Requirements
Navy print	3¼ yards
Dark green print	1 yard
Purple print	½ yard
Assorted light prints	1¾ yards
Assorted medium prints	½ yard
Assorted dark prints	2¾ yards
Backing	5¼ yards
Navy print for bias binding	1 yard

Pieces to Cut
Navy print
    2 (9½" x 60½") border strips
    2 (9½" x 87½") border strips
    26 E
    26 E rev.
    22 I
    26 J
    2 K
    2 K rev.

Dark green print
    48 C
    26 D
Purple print
    26 E
    26 E rev.
Assorted light prints
    120 B
    170 E*
    170 E rev.*
    232 G*
Assorted medium prints
    30 A
    58 F
Assorted dark prints
    120 C*
    85 D
    232 H*
*Cut 4 from each print.

Quilt Top Assembly

1. Following Block 1 Assembly Diagram, join 1 medium print A, 4 light print Bs, and 4 dark print Cs to make 1 Block 1. Repeat to make 30 Block 1s.

Following Block 2 Assembly Diagram, join 1 dark print D to 4 light print Es to make 1 Block 2. Repeat to make 85 Block 2s.

Following Block 3 Assembly Diagram, join 1 medium print F, 4 light print Gs, and 4 dark print Hs to make 1 Block 3. Repeat to make 58 Block 3s.

Following Block 4 Assembly Diagram, join 1 navy print I, 2 dark green print Cs, and 1 navy print J to make 1 Block 4. Repeat to make 22 Block 4s.

Following Block 5 Assembly Diagram, join 1 dark green D, 2 purple print Es, and 2 navy print Es to make 1 Block 5. Repeat to make 26 Block 5s.

Following Corner Block 1 Assembly Diagram, join 1 navy print K rev., 1 dark green C, and 1 navy print J to make 1 Corner Block 1. Repeat to make 2 Corner Block 1s.

Following Corner Block 2 Assembly Diagram, join 1 navy print K, 1 dark green C, and 1 navy print J to make 1 Corner Block 2. Repeat to make 2 Corner Block 2s.

2. Following Quilt Top Assembly Diagram and referring to photograph for color placement, join 6 Block 2s and 7 Block 3s to make 1 Row 1. Repeat to make 6 Row 1s.

In same manner, join 6 Block 1s and 7 Block 2s to make 1 Row 2. Repeat to make 5 Row 2s. Join rows.

3. To make 1 side pieced border, join 6 Block 4s and 7 Block 5s as shown in Quilt Top Assembly Diagram. Repeat to make second side pieced border. Join to sides of quilt.

To make top pieced border, join 5 Block 4s and 6 Block 5s as shown in Quilt Top Assembly Diagram. Join 1 Corner Block 2 to left end of pieced border. Join 1 Corner Block 1 to right end of pieced border. In same manner, join 5 Block 4s, 6 Block 5s, 1 Corner Block 1, and 1 Corner Block 2 to make bottom pieced border. Join to top and bottom of quilt as shown, butting corners.

4. Join 9½" x 60½" navy print border strips to top and bottom of quilt. Join 9½" x 87½" navy print border strips to sides of quilt, butting corners.

5. To complete outer border, join 7 Block 2s and 8 Block 3s in L shape, as shown in Quilt Top Assembly Diagram. Align outer raw edges of pieced strip with outer edges of navy print border; appliqué inner edges to border. Repeat.

Quilting

Quilt in-the-ditch around all pieces. Quilt navy print border as desired.

Finished Edges

Bind with bias binding made from navy print fabric.

Block Assembly Diagrams

Corner Block 1—Make 2.

Corner Block 2—Make 2.

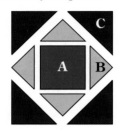

Block 1—Make 30.

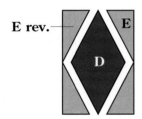

Block 2—Make 85.

Block 3—Make 58.

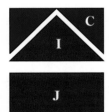

Block 4—Make 22.

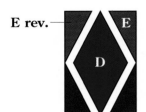

Block 5—Make 26.

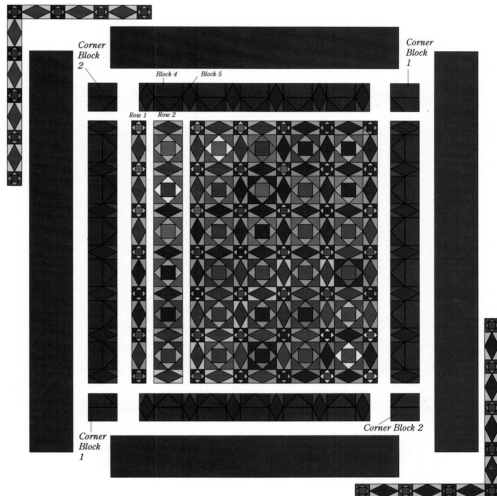

Quilt Top Assembly Diagram

79

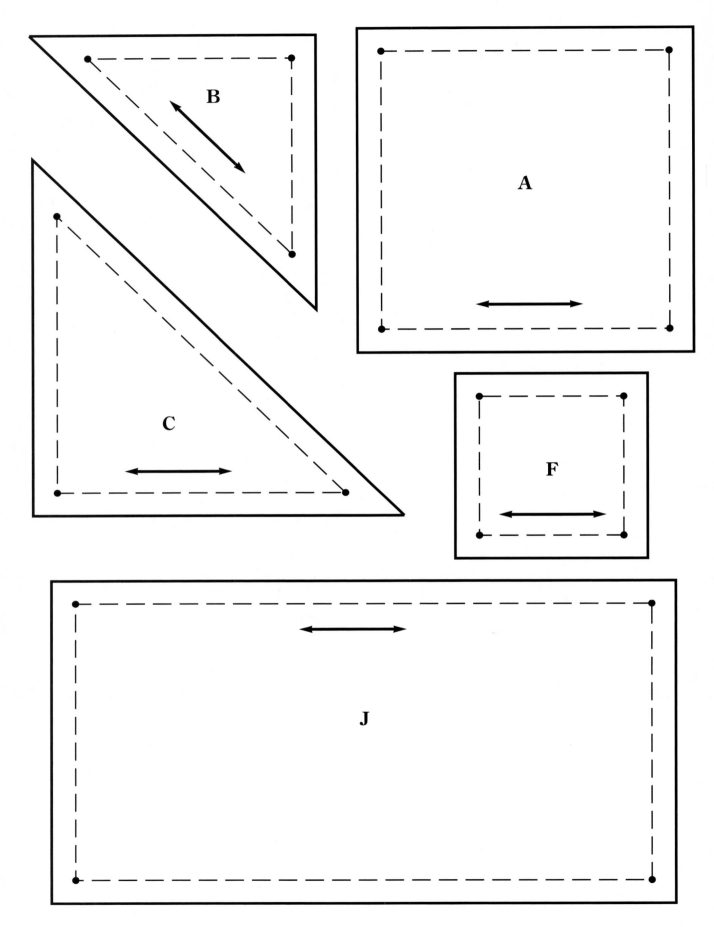

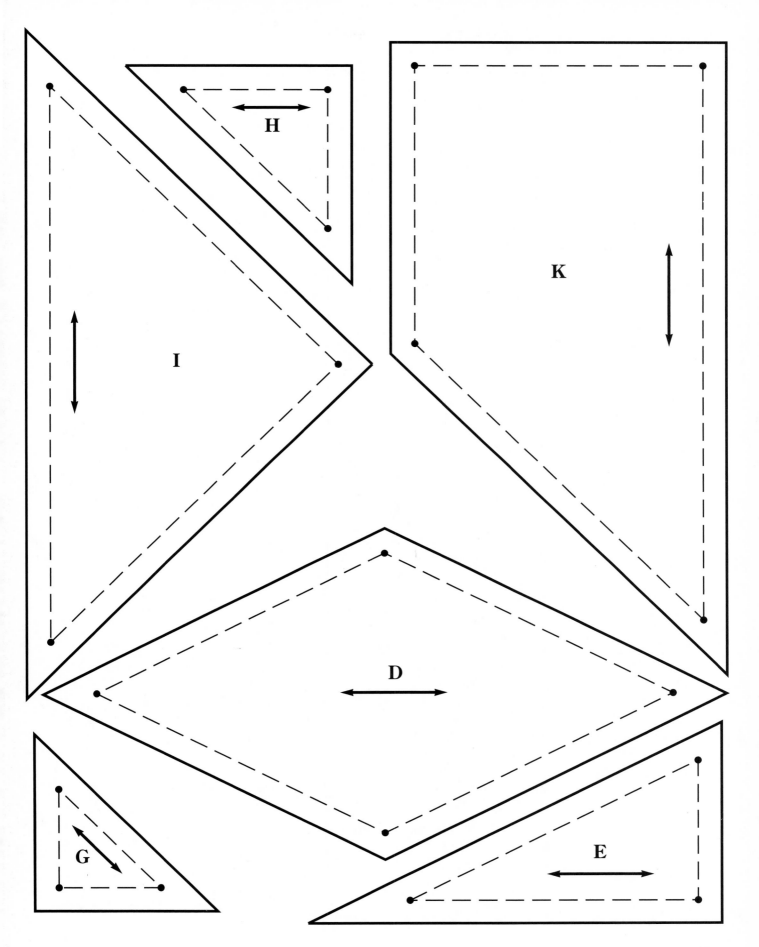

H

K

I

D

G

E

"I have a nice collection of jackets and vests that I've been making recently. I've found that making quilts to wear is faster than making bed quilts, and just as much fun!"

Barbara Tricarico
VIENNA, VIRGINIA

Barbara Tricarico's life is filled with quilts! She is currently president of her 1,000-member guild, Quilters Unlimited of Northern Virginia, as well as past president of her local chapter, the Vienna Quilters Unlimited. She also is active in the Night Owls Bee, a 40-member group that meets weekly, and in a 12-member fiber arts group called FiberKinesis that acts as a critique group for the members' fiber arts projects.

Although guild officers and organizers sometimes have little time to actually spend making quilts, Barbara makes time for that as well. "Lately I've been concentrating on quilted clothing," she says. "My walls are filling up with quilts, so now I'm wearing my work instead of hanging it!"

Vienna Stars
1990

Vienna Stars was Barbara's response to a challenge sponsored by her guild, the Vienna Quilters Unlimited. The challenge kit contained six fabrics, of which each quilter was required to use four; adding up to four additional fabrics was also permitted. The finished project was to be a wall hanging using any pattern of the quilter's choice.

Barbara used all six of the challenge fabrics, adding two more prints for flowers and the white-on-white print for the background. The star block she used for the center was drafted from a photograph of an antique crib quilt she had seen in a *Country Living* magazine. The floral appliqué border is an original design that Barbara added to soften the geometric center blocks.

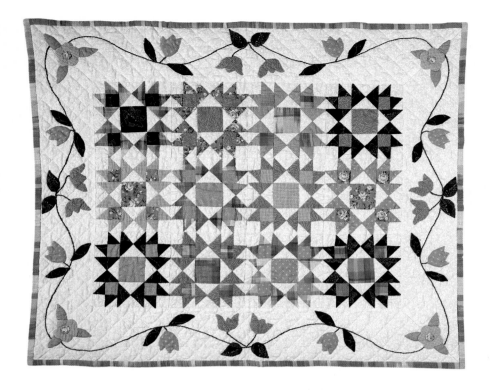

Quilt Top Assembly

1. Following Block Assembly Diagram, join 1 dark print A, 8 white-on-white print Bs, 8 light print Bs, 4 dark print Cs, 4 white-on-white print Cs, 8 dark print Ds, and 8 white-on-white print Ds to make 1 block. Repeat to make 12 blocks.

2. Join blocks in 4 rows of 3 blocks each. Join rows.

3. Join 5¼" x 34" white-on-white print border strips to top and bottom of quilt. Join 5¼" x 28" white-on-white print border strips to sides of quilt, mitering corners.

4. Referring to Quilt Top Assembly Diagram for placement, appliqué flowers and leaves to borders as shown. Using 3 strands of floss, outline-stitch vines and stems.

Quilting

Quilt all block pieces in-the-ditch. Outline-quilt all appliqué pieces. Quilt border with ¾" cross-hatch pattern. Or quilt as desired.

Finished Edges

Bind with bias binding made from pink plaid.

Vienna Stars

Finished Quilt Size
33½" x 27½"

Number of Blocks and Finished Size
12 blocks   6" x 6"

Fabric Requirements
White-on-white print   1¼ yards
Assorted dark prints   ¼ yard
   or 12 (6") squares
Assorted light prints   ½ yard
   or 12 (10") squares
Pink print   ⅛ yard
Blue print   ⅛ yard
Dark green print   ⅛ yard
Pink plaid   ⅛ yard
Pink floral   scrap
Light green print   ⅛ yard
Backing   1 yard
Pink plaid
   for bias binding   ½ yard
Dark green embroidery floss

Pieces to Cut
White-on-white print
   2 (5¼" x 34") border strips
   2 (5¼" x 28") border strips
   96 B
   48 C
   96 D

Assorted dark prints
   12 A*
   48 C*
Assorted light prints
   96 B**
   96 D**
Pink print
   8 E
   8 F
   8 F rev.
Blue print
   8 H
Dark green print
   16 I
Pink plaid
   4 J
Pink floral
   4 K
Light green print
   12 L
*Cut 1 A and 4 Cs of same print.
**Cut 8 Bs and 8 Ds of same print.

Block Assembly Diagram

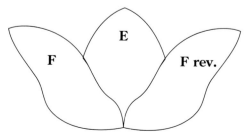

Tulip Appliqué Diagram

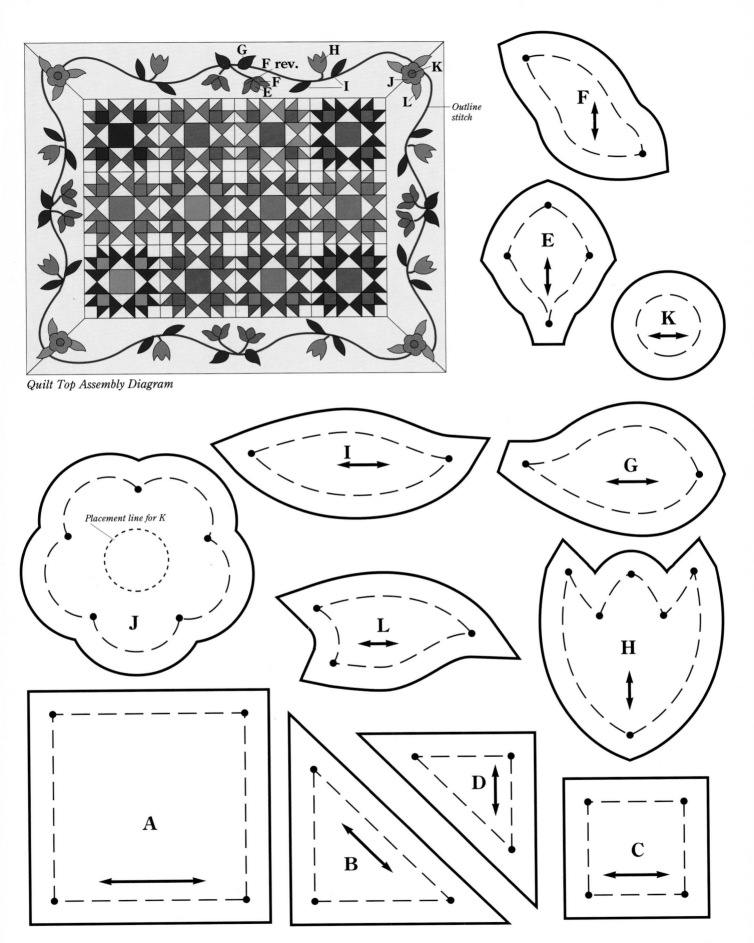

Quilt Top Assembly Diagram

85

"Quilting is a lifeline from past generations to the present."

Carol Butzke
SLINGER, WISCONSIN

"I enjoy the challenge that different quilt styles have to offer," Carol Butzke says, describing the type of quilt she prefers to make. "I've made appliquéd, pieced, pictorial, Hawaiian-style, and Amish-style quilts."

An expert quiltmaker, Carol has completed more than 50 pieces since she began quilting in 1980, and many of her traditional-with-a-twist quilts have won awards. The most recent honor went to her quilt *Delectable Mountains,* which won the first place award in Traditional Pieced Quilts, Large, Professional Category, at the 1994 American Quilter's Society show in Paducah, Kentucky. This prize is a purchase award, meaning that the quilt becomes part of the permanent collection of the Museum of the American Quilter's Society.

"Quilting fulfills a need for creative expression in my life," Carol says.

Visions of Santa Danced in My Head
1992

"I decorate heavily during each Christmas season," Carol says. "Two 7½' trees are just the start. This quilt became an extension of my collection of Victorian Father Christmas cards and the ornaments I made based on those cards."

Visions of Santa Danced in My Head is a friendship quilt made from blocks stitched by Carol's fellow members in the Kettle Moraine Quilters and It's a Stitch Quilt Club. Carol provided the block patterns (which she adapted from a soft sculpture Santa doll by Susan Tinker), the fabric for the background squares, and fabric for the coats and faces. "The rest," Carol says, "was the result of the ingenuity of each participant." One Santa carries a Statue of Liberty in his sack, a reference to Carol's 1986 quilt *Bright Hopes,*

Bright Promise, which represented Wisconsin in the Great American Quilt Festival honoring the centennial anniversary of the Statue of Liberty.

Carol's two sons take turns using the quilt each Christmas season. "Hopefully," Carol says, "it will live out its life, in this generation and the next, as part of our family's Christmas tradition."

Visions of Santa Danced in My Head

Finished Quilt Size
96" x 96"

Number of Blocks and Finished Size
25 blocks   12" x 12"

Fabric Requirements
Dark green	2¾ yards
Light green	2 yards
Red	2½ yards
White	3¼ yards
Black	¼ yard
Peach	⅛ yard
"Fur"*	½ yard
Assorted solids	1¼ yards
Assorted prints	¾ yard
Backing	8¾ yards
Dark green for bias binding	1 yard

Black embroidery floss
*"Fur" may be fake fur, fleece, or other fabric suitable for trim and beard.

Pieces to Cut
Dark green
    4 (4½" x 96½") outer border strips
    3 (16¾") squares**
    2 (8⅞") squares†

Light green
    32 W
Red
    4 (1¼" x 88½") inner border strips
    128 (1¼" x 13¼") block border
        strips
    240 X
    24 Y
White
    25 (12½") background squares
Black
    25 A (boot)
    25 B (boot)
Peach
    25 O (face)
"Fur"
    25 D (coat trim)
    25 E (coat trim)
    25 G (cuff)
    25 M (cuff)
    25 P (hat trim)
    25 Q (beard)
Assorted solids
    16 C (coat)
    25 F (mitten)
    16 K (sleeve for coat C)††
    25 L (mitten)
    9 U (coat)
    25 N (hat)‡
Assorted prints
    8 H (gift)
    8 I (gift)

8 J (bag)
9 R (gift)
9 S (gift)
9 T (basket)
8 V (wreath)
**Cut squares into quarters diagonally for 12 side triangles.
† Cut squares in half diagonally for 4 corner triangles.
††Cut sleeve K from same fabric as coat C.
‡ For each block, cut hat from same fabric as coat.

Quilt Top Assembly

1. To make appliqué placement guidelines, fold 1 white background square in half diagonally and finger-press. Unfold square; fold in half along opposite diagonal and finger-press. Unfold. Repeat to mark all background squares.

2. Following Bag Santa Appliqué Placement Diagram, appliqué pieces to 1 background square in this order: 1 A, 1 B, 1 C, 1 D, 1 E, 1 F, 1 G, 1 H, 1 I, 1 J, 1 K, 1 L, 1 M, 1 N, 1 O, 1 Q, and 1 P. Using 2 strands of black embroidery floss, outline-stitch eyebrows, nose, mustache, and ribbons on gifts H and I. Satin-stitch eyes to make 1 Bag Santa block. Repeat to make 8 Bag Santa blocks.

3. Following Wreath Santa Appliqué Placement Diagram, appliqué pieces to 1 background square in this order: 1 A, 1 B, 1 C, 1 D, 1 E, 1 F, 1 G, 1 N, 1 O, 1 Q, 1 P, 1 K, 1 V, 1 L, and 1 M. Using 2 strands of black embroidery floss, outline-stitch eyebrows, nose, and mustache. Satin-stitch eyes to make 1 Wreath Santa block. Repeat to make 8 Wreath Santa blocks.

4. Following Basket Santa Appliqué Placement Diagram, appliqué pieces to 1 background square in this order: 1 A, 1 B, 1 U, 1 D, 1 E, 1 F, 1 G, 1 N, 1 O, 1 Q, 1 P, 1 R, 1 S, 1 T, 1 L, and 1 M. Using 2 strands of black embroidery floss, outline-stitch eyebrows, nose, mustache, ribbons on gifts R and S, and band on basket T. Satin-stitch eyes to make 1 Basket Santa block. Repeat to make 9 Basket Santa blocks.

5. Around each completed block, join 4 (1¼" x 13¼") red block border strips in log cabin fashion as shown in Block Border Strip Diagram.

6. To make sashing strips, join red Xs to each end of light green Ws as shown in Sashing Strip Assembly Diagram and Quilt Top Assembly Diagram.

7. Join blocks, side triangles, corner triangles, remaining block border strips, sashing strips, and red sashing squares Y in diagonal rows as shown in Quilt Top Assembly Diagram. Join rows.

8. Join 2 (1¼" x 88½") red inner border strips to top and bottom of quilt. Join remaining red inner border strips to sides of quilt, mitering corners. Join 2 (4½" x 96½") dark green outer border strips to top and bottom of quilt. Join remaining dark green outer border strips to sides of quilt, mitering corners.

Quilting

Outline-quilt appliqué figures. Quilt 1½" cross-hatch pattern on remainder of each block and on each side triangle and corner triangle. Quilt block border strips and sashing strips in-the-ditch. Quilt outer border as desired.

Finished Edges

Bind with bias binding made from dark green fabric.

Bag Santa Appliqué Placement Diagram Make 8.

Wreath Santa Appliqué Placement Diagram Make 8.

Basket Santa Appliqué Placement Diagram Make 9.

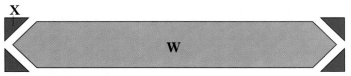

Sashing Strip Assembly Diagram

Block Border Strip Diagram

Quilt Top Assembly Diagram

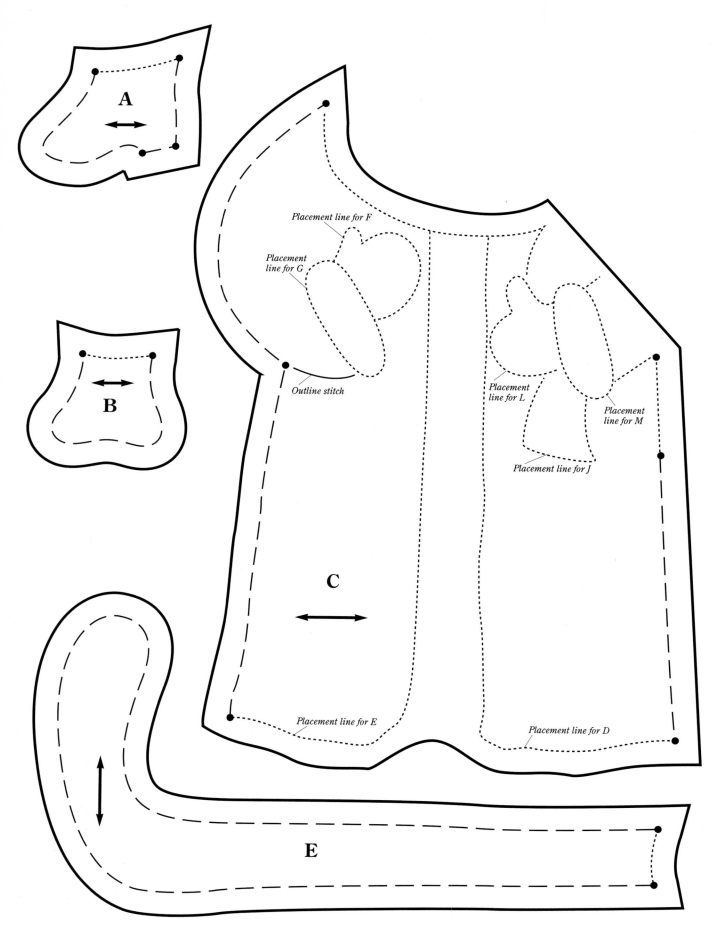

A

B

C

E

Placement line for F

Placement line for G

Outline stitch

Placement line for L

Placement line for M

Placement line for J

Placement line for E

Placement line for D

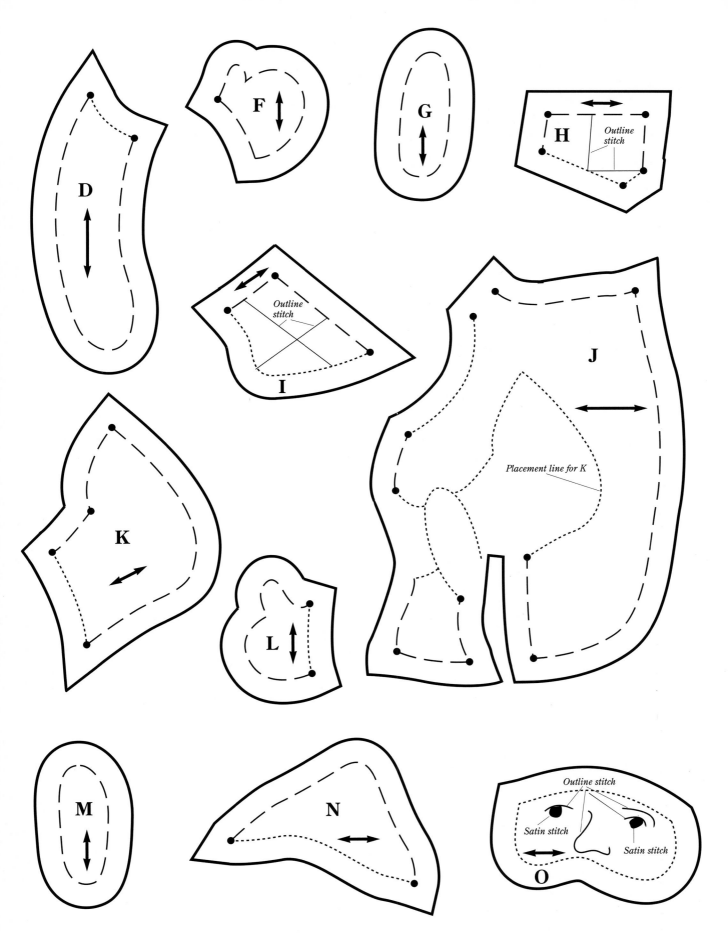

D

F

G

H
Outline
stitch

Outline
stitch
I

J

Placement line for K

K

L

M

N

O
Outline stitch
Satin stitch
Satin stitch

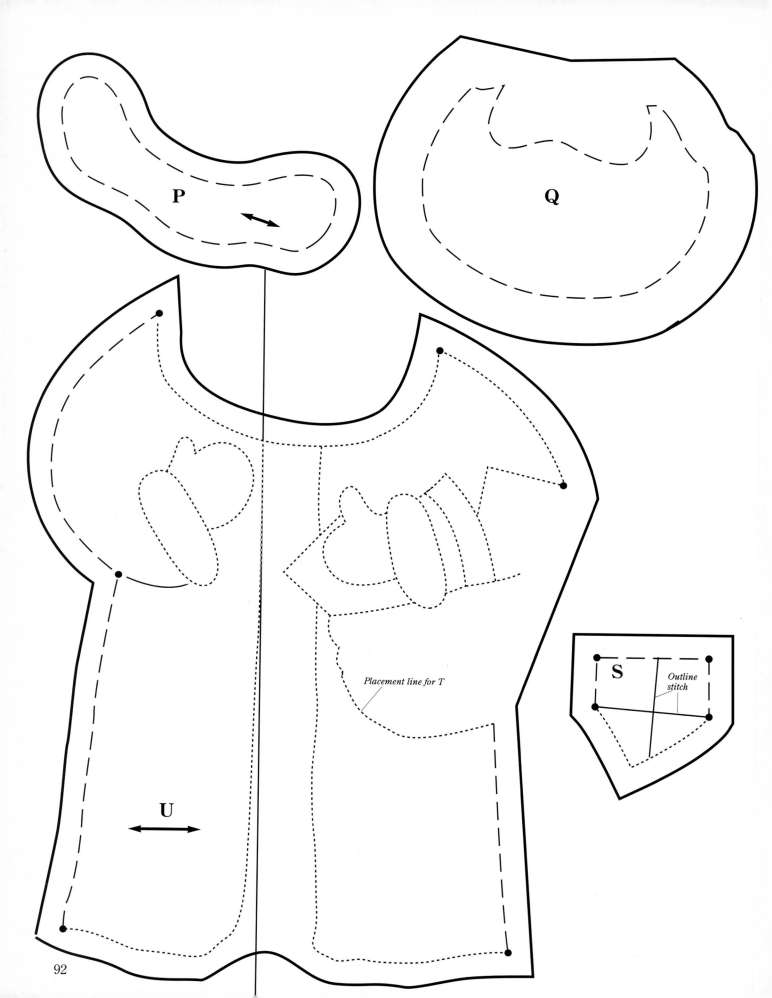

P

Q

Placement line for T

S

Outline stitch

U

92

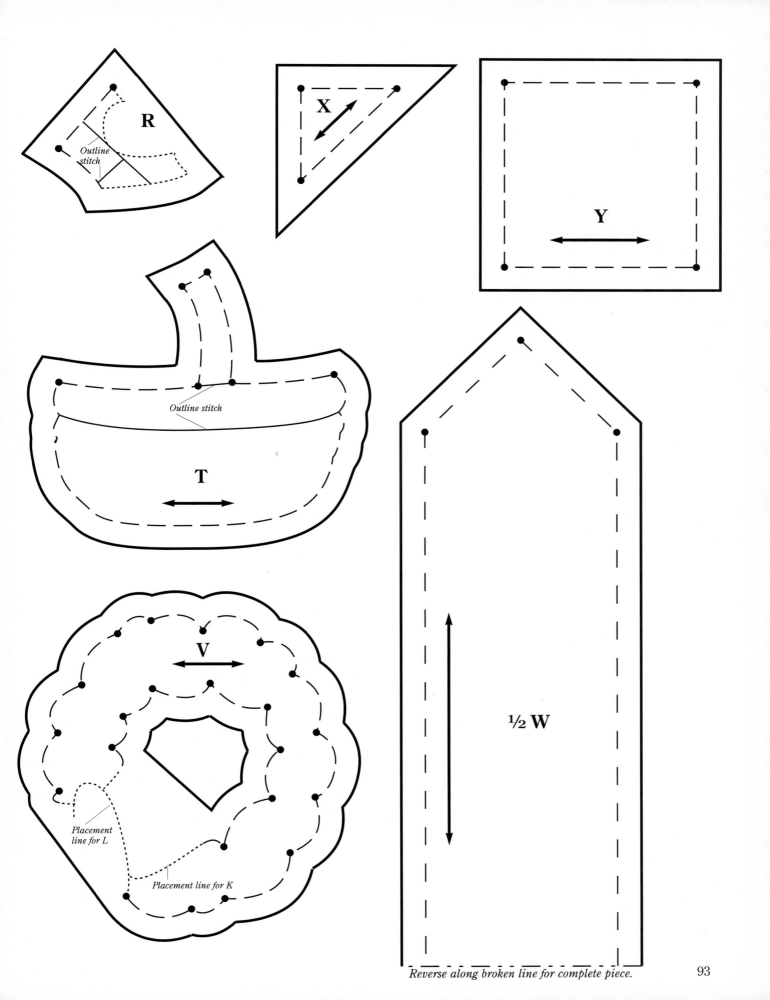

R

Outline stitch

X

Y

Outline stitch

T

½ W

V

Placement line for L

Placement line for K

Reverse along broken line for complete piece.

93

"I love intricate work. I did a quilt this year that had 6,005 pieces and took five spools of quilting thread!"

Pauline Bryant
McALESTER, OKLAHOMA

When Pauline Bryant was 8 years old, she made her first quilt, a small one for her dolls. That was the beginning of a love affair with quilting that has lasted ever since.

"I couldn't devote much time to it while our children were growing up," she says, "but in 1978 I quit work and began making quilts in earnest."

Pauline has completed about 50 quilts for herself and her family and has quilted almost that many tops for other people. Her exquisite stitches have brought her a number of awards at state and county fairs, including seven first-place ribbons and one Best of Show.

Oklahoma Dogwood
1992

"I enjoyed every minute of the 245 hours of work this quilt required," Pauline says. "I chose the pattern for *Oklahoma Dogwood* because of the challenge of hand-piecing the tiny pieces in each block. I also love to do intricate hand quilting because of the beauty of the stitches. "

Memories of Pauline's youngest brother, who died shortly after the quilt was finished, are also part of *Oklahoma Dogwood*. "He loved to watch me work on this quilt," says Pauline, "and the day I took it out of the frame, he was as happy as I was. He insisted that I enter it in the 1992 Oklahoma State Fair. Despite the fact that he was so ill, he even drove me to Oklahoma City—a distance of 140 miles—so that I could enter it. He was so thrilled that it won both the blue ribbon for pieced quilts and Best of Show. I'm glad that he lived to see it."

mauve solid Fs as shown to make 1 Unit 1. Repeat to make 8 Unit 1s.

Following Block 1 Unit 2 Assembly Diagram, join 4 mauve print As, 4 burgundy print As, 2 burgundy print Bs, 2 burgundy print Cs, 2 burgundy print C revs, 10 mauve print Ds, 8 burgundy print Es, and 2 mauve solid Fs as shown to make 1 Unit 2. Repeat to make 8 Unit 2s.

To make 1 Block 1, join 2 Unit 1s and 2 Unit 2s as shown in Block 1 Assembly Diagram. Repeat to make 4 Block 1s.

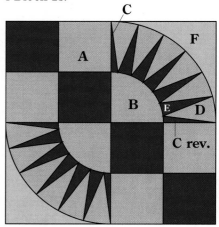

Block 1 Unit 1—Make 8.

Block 1 Unit 2—Make 8.

2. Following Block 2 Assembly Diagram, join 4 mauve print As, 4 burgundy print As, 4 mauve print Bs, 4 burgundy print Bs, and 4 mauve solid Gs as shown to make 1 Block 2. Repeat to make 11 Block 2s.

3. Following Border Block Assembly Diagram, join 2 mauve print As, 2 burgundy print As, and 4 mauve solid Hs to make 1 Border Block. Repeat to make 68 Border Blocks. Set aside.

Oklahoma Dogwood

Finished Quilt Size
85" x 95"

Number of Blocks and Finished Size
4 Block 1s	14" x 14"
11 Block 2s	7½" x 7½"

Fabric Requirements
Mauve solid	5¼ yards
Mauve print	2½ yards
Burgundy print	2½ yards
Backing	7¾ yards
Burgundy print for bias binding	1 yard

Pieces to Cut
Mauve solid
  2 (3¼" x 85½") border strips
  2 (3¼" x 75½") border strips
  2 (31⅛") squares*
  12 (8" x 14½") sashing strips
  1 (11⅞") square**
  32 F
  44 G
  272 H

Mauve print
  2 (2¾" x 85½") border strips
  2 (2¾" x 75½") border strips
  244 A
  60 B
  160 D

Burgundy print
  2 (2½" x 85½") border strips
  2 (2½" x 75½") border strips
  244 A
  60 B
  32 C
  32 C rev.
  128 E

*Cut each square in half diagonally for 4 corner triangles.

**Cut into quarters diagonally; discard 2 quarters for 2 side triangles.

Quilt Top Assembly

1. For help in piecing curves, refer to Quilt Smart, "Piecing Curves," on page 12. Following Block 1 Unit 1 Assembly Diagram, join 4 mauve print As, 4 burgundy print As, 2 mauve print Bs, 2 burgundy print Cs, 2 burgundy print C revs, 10 mauve print Ds, 8 burgundy print Es, and 2

Unit 1   Unit 2

Unit 2   Unit 1

Block 1 Assembly Diagram—Make 4.

Block 2 Assembly Diagram—Make 11.

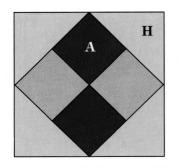

Border Block Assembly Diagram—Make 68.

4. To make center medallion, join 4 Block 1s, 7 Block 2s, 8" x 14½" mauve solid sashing strips, and side triangles as shown in Quilt Top Assembly Diagram on page 98, appliquéing loose corners of Block 2s to sashing strips.

5. Join corner triangles to center medallion. Appliqué loose corners of Block 2s to corner triangles as shown. Appliqué remaining Block 2s.

6. To make inner top border, join 1 (3¼" x 75½") mauve solid border strip, 1 (2¾" x 75½") mauve print border strip, and 1 (2½" x 75½") burgundy print border strip along long edges. Join to quilt with burgundy print strip adjacent to top, matching center of border to center of quilt. Repeat to make inner bottom border; join to quilt in same manner.

To make 1 inner side border, join 1 (3¼" x 85½") mauve solid border strip, 1 (2¾" x 85½") mauve print border strip, and 1 (2½" x 85½") burgundy print border strip along long edges. Repeat to make second side border. Join borders to quilt with burgundy print strip adjacent to top, mitering corners.

7. To make top pieced border, join 15 Border Blocks with burgundy print As on sides of blocks, as shown in Quilt Top Assembly Diagram. Repeat to make bottom pieced border. Join to top and bottom of quilt.

To make 1 side pieced border, join 19 Border Blocks in same manner. Repeat to make second side pieced border. Join to sides of quilt, butting corners.

Quilting

Outline-quilt all pieces in Blocks 1 and 2 and Border Blocks. Quilt 1" cross-hatch pattern in corner triangles. Quilt borders and sashing strips as desired.

Finished Edges

Bind with bias binding made from burgundy print fabric.

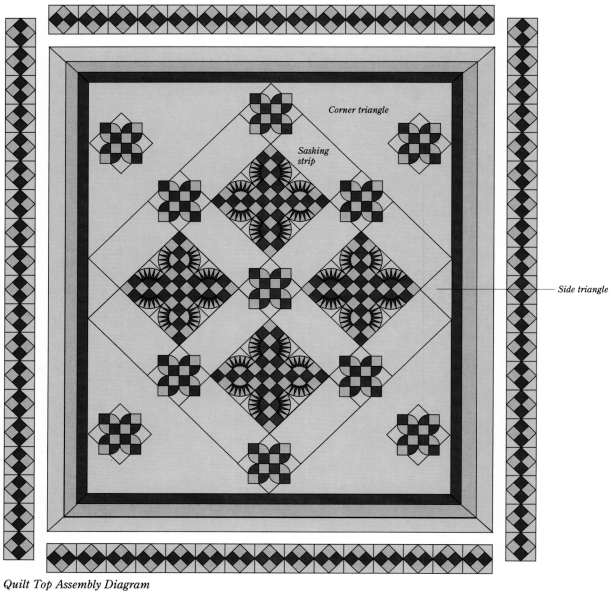

Corner triangle

Sashing strip

Side triangle

Quilt Top Assembly Diagram

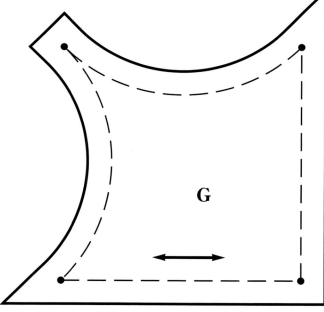

G

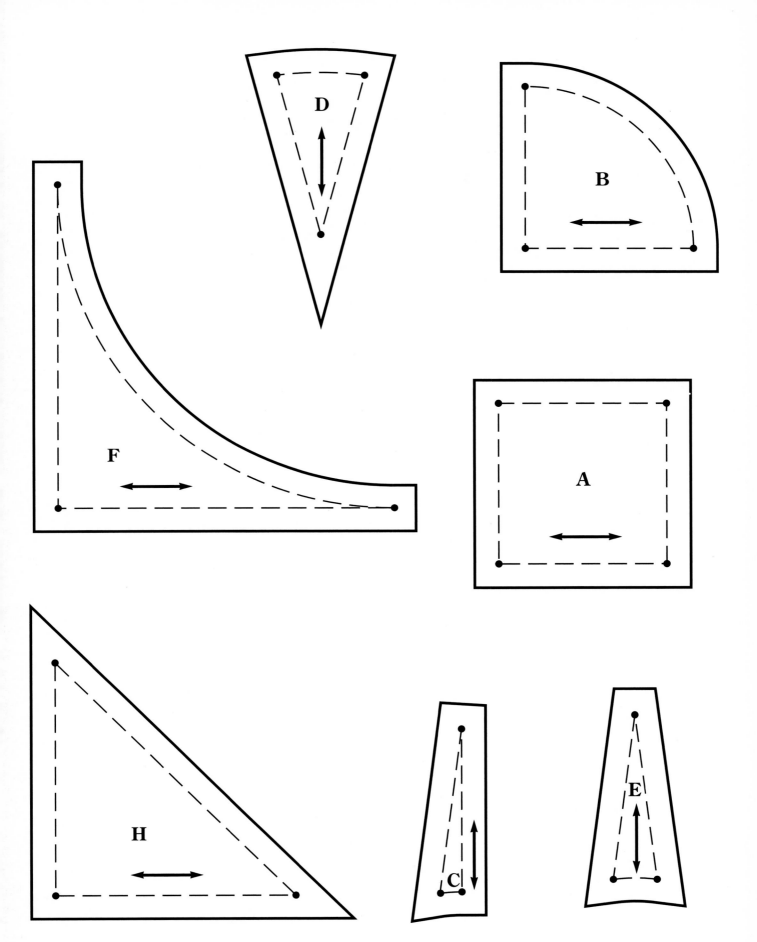

Nancy Kasper
SAN ANTONIO, TEXAS

"I learned to sew from a friend when I was 16," Nancy Kasper says, "but I didn't start quilting until I was expecting my first child." Primarily self-taught, Nancy found that her skills improved rapidly when she joined the Greater San Antonio Quilt Guild. "In a guild, I get to see other people's techniques and watch as they complete their quilts," she says. "It's really helped me to get better."

Nancy's favorite part of quiltmaking lies in quilting each completed piece. "Although I really enjoy hand piecing, I enjoy hand quilting the most," she says. "That's when I pour my heart and soul into every last stitch."

Granny's Favorite
1991

Nancy took the pattern for this quilt from one made by her great-grandmother, Nannie Stewart Taylor, about 1920. Although Nannie Taylor called the pattern Evening Star, Nancy named her quilt *Granny's Favorite* in honor of her ancestor. "I wanted to make a quilt for my mother, one that would preserve my great-grandmother's pattern," Nancy says. "Needless to say, my mom was in tears when she opened the box and saw the new quilt just for her!"

Assorted medium prints
  80 A
Assorted light prints
  80 A
*Cut into quarters diagonally; discard 2
  for 14 side triangles.

Quilt Top Assembly
  1. For help in piecing curves, refer
to Quilt Smart, "Piecing Curves," on
page 12. Following Block Assembly
Diagram, join 4 medium print As, 4
light print As, 8 dark print Bs, 4
muslin Cs, and 4 muslin Ds to make
1 block. Repeat to make 20 blocks.
  2. Join blocks in diagonal rows
with setting squares and side triangles as shown in Quilt Top Assembly
Diagram. Join rows.

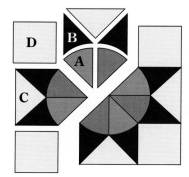

Block Assembly Diagram

Granny's Favorite

Finished Quilt Size
71" x 88½"

**Number of Blocks and
Finished Size**
20 blocks   12½" x 12½"

Fabric Requirements
Muslin   4½ yards
Assorted dark prints   2¼ yards
Assorted medium prints   1 yard
Assorted light prints   1 yard
Backing   5½ yards
Muslin
  for bias binding   1 yard

Pieces to Cut
Muslin
  12 (13") setting squares
  4 (19") squares*
  80 C
  80 D
Assorted dark prints
  160 B

Quilting
  Outline-quilt pieces in star blocks.
Quilt setting squares with Feather
Wreath (pattern on page 33).

Finished Edges
  Bind with bias binding made from
muslin.

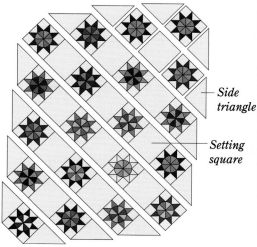

— *Side
triangle*

— *Setting
square*

Quilt Top Assembly Diagram

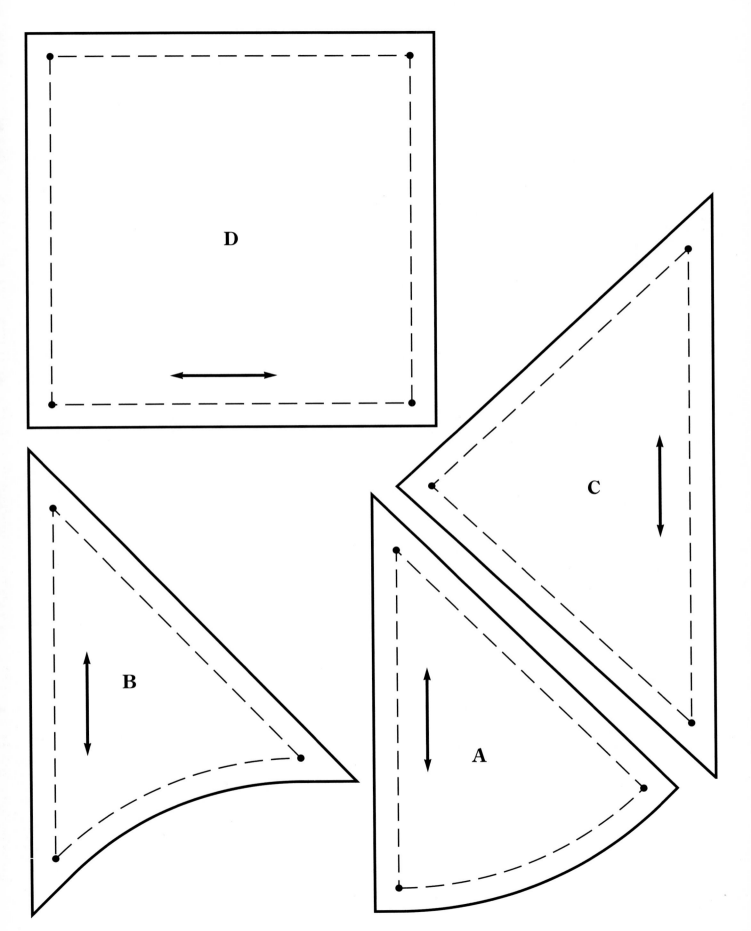

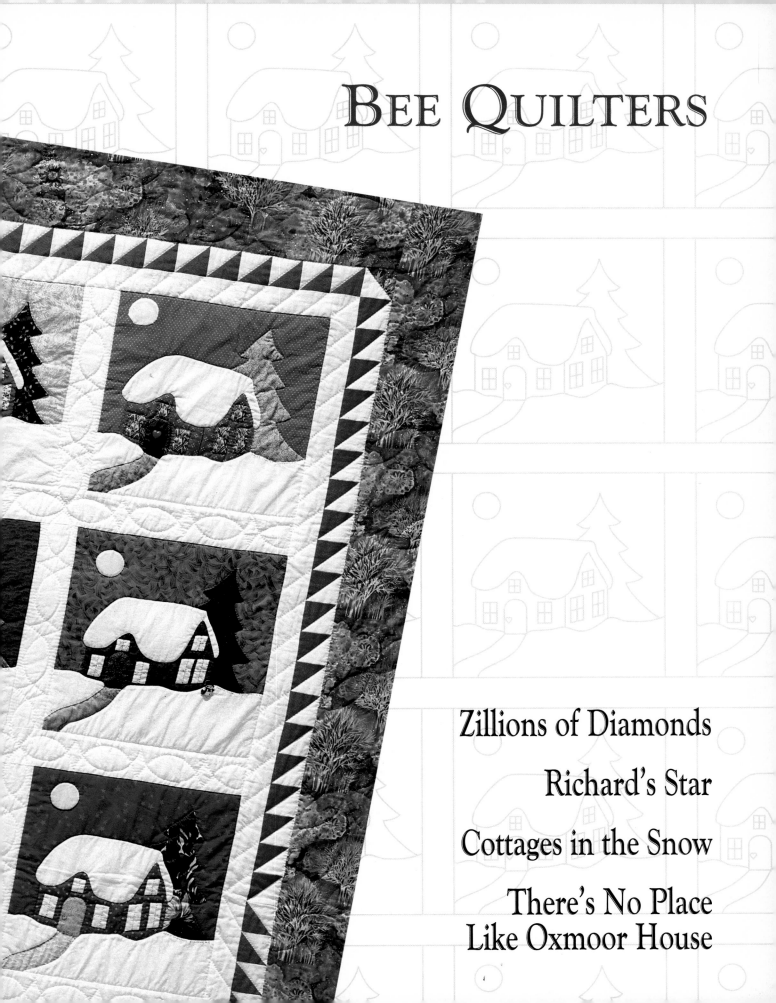

BEE QUILTERS

Zillions of Diamonds

Richard's Star

Cottages in the Snow

There's No Place
Like Oxmoor House

Front row (L to R): Mary Ann Schmidt, Shirley Butts, Susan Ennis, Nancy Roth, Nancy Grove. Back row (L to R): Ruth Reiber, Flo Cox, Wanda Pattersen, Barbara Caves, Joyce Horne, Cindra Landon, Crissa Landon.

"We don't know what our next quilt project will be. We just know the design won't contain any diamonds!"

Mountain Mavericks
MORRISON, COLORADO

The Mountain Mavericks are a group of 10 talented quiltmakers living in the Front Range Mountain area of Colorado. The women who make up the Mavericks are diverse in age, interests, and backgrounds, but all are dedicated to learning new techniques and creating innovative designs in the quilts they make together. "We like to experiment with different techniques for every quilt we do," says Mary Ann Schmidt, the Mavericks' group leader. "Our emphasis is on learning, sharing, and supporting individual members of the group."

One of the Mountain Mavericks' group quilts has been exhibited in Japan, and *Zillions of Diamonds* was exhibited at the Colorado Capitol Quilt Show in 1992.

Zillions of Diamonds
1992

Zillions of Diamonds had its beginnings in an earlier quilt by the Mountain Mavericks that required a perfect Colorado sky color. To achieve that color, the guild members experimented with dyeing fabric and had so much fun they didn't want to stop. "The idea of making a glowing star quilt using a monochromatic color scheme evolved as we went along," says Mary Ann Schmidt. The group experimented with Procion dyes on muslin, varying a number of factors to create the light, medium, and dark values finally used in the quilt you see here. (See "Resources" for infor-

mation on supplies for fabric dyeing.)

"The border became the final design challenge," Mary Ann says. "There was so much outward movement that we wanted to contain it without stifling the excitement." The careful placement of values in the three borders achieved the desired effect.

From fabric dyeing through meticulous hand piecing to final quilting, *Zillions of Diamonds* took two years to complete. "We don't know what our next quilt project will be," Mary Ann laughs. "We just know the design won't contain any diamonds!"

Zillions of Diamonds

Finished Quilt Size
84¾" x 84¾"

Fabric Requirements
Assorted light solids   4¾ yards
Assorted medium solids 5¾ yards
Assorted dark solids   3¼ yards
Backing   7¾ yards
Dark fabric
    for bias binding   1 yard

Pieces to Cut
Assorted light solids
    12 (2⅜"-wide) crosswise strips
    104 A
    496 B
    792 C
Assorted medium solids
    12 (2⅜"-wide) crosswise strips
    400 A
    304 B
Assorted dark solids
    12 (2⅜"-wide) crosswise strips
    32 A
    64 B
    792 C

Quilt Top Assembly
1. Referring to Diamond Assembly Diagram, make indicated number of each pieced diamond unit using Bs and Cs. (Be sure to carefully follow color values shown in each unit diagram.)

2. Referring to Quilt Top Assembly Diagram, Figure 1, join As and pieced units into rows as shown. Join rows. Repeat to make 4 right-hand triangles.

Referring to Quilt Top Assembly Diagram, Figure 2, join remaining As and pieced units in same manner to make 4 left-hand triangles.

Trim each triangle as shown in Quilt Top Assembly Diagram, Figure 3, on page 110. Join triangles, alternating right-hand and left-hand triangles, as shown in Quilt Top Assembly Diagram, Figure 4, on page 111.

3. To make pieced border, cut 12 (2⅜"-wide) light solid strips into random lengths. Using template made from diamond A for guide, cut each end to 45° angle. Join strips along 45° cuts, varying colors, to make 1 long strip. (Refer to photograph for example of color variation.) Cut into 4 (85½"-long) pieced strips. Repeat to make 4 (85½"-long) strips from medium solids and 4 (85½"-long) strips from dark solids.

Join 1 light, 1 medium, and 1 dark pieced strip to make 1 pieced border.

Repeat to make 4 borders. With light strip adjacent to quilt top, join borders to sides of quilt, mitering corners.

Quilting
Quilt in-the-ditch around each diamond unit. Quilt borders in-the-ditch between light, medium, and dark pieced strips.

Finished Edges
Bind with bias binding made from dark fabric.

Diamond Assembly Diagram

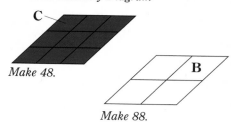

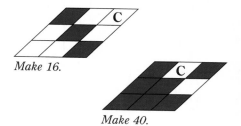

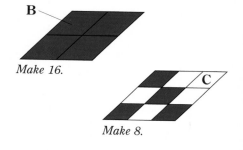

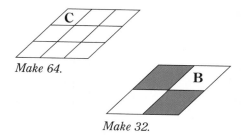

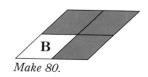

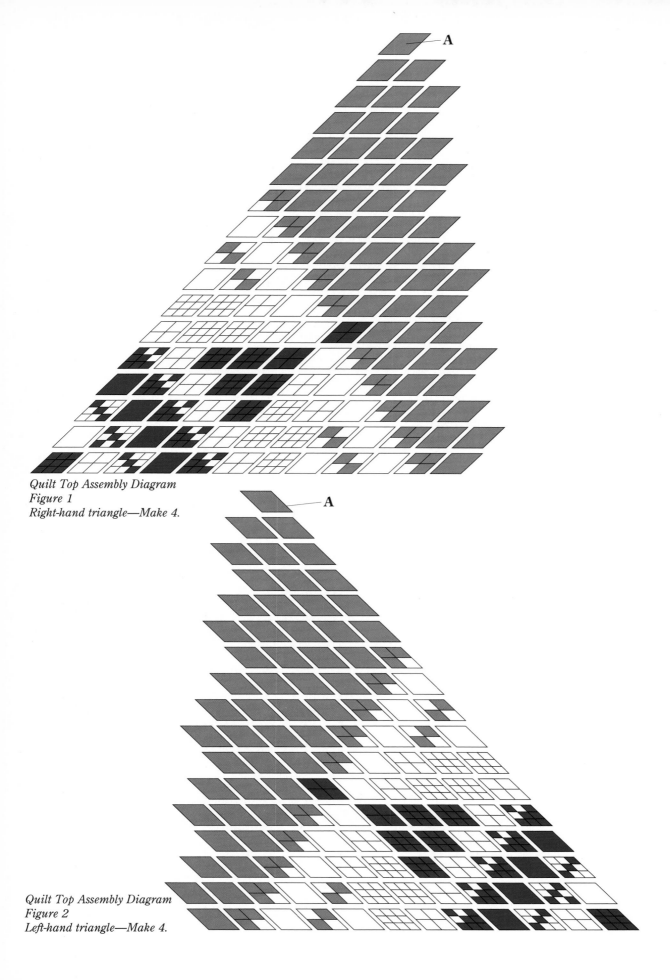

Quilt Top Assembly Diagram
Figure 1
Right-hand triangle—Make 4.

Quilt Top Assembly Diagram
Figure 2
Left-hand triangle—Make 4.

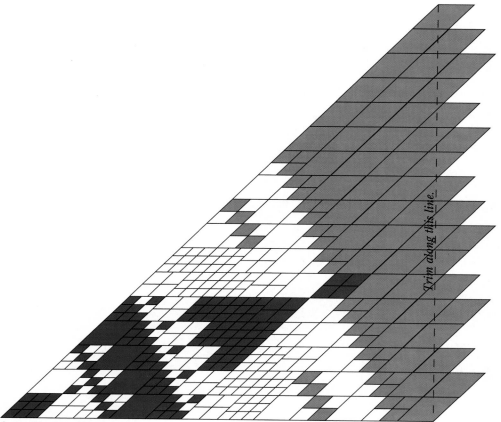

Trim along this line.

Quilt Top Assembly Diagram
Figure 3

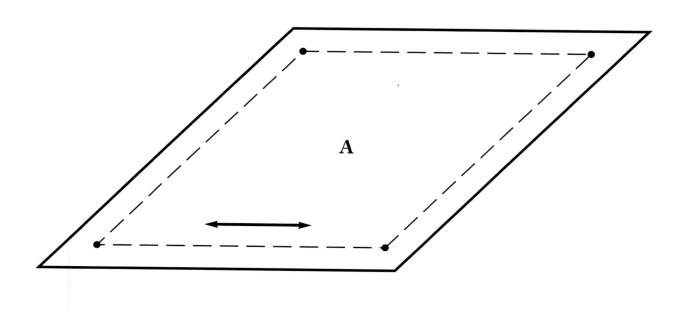

A

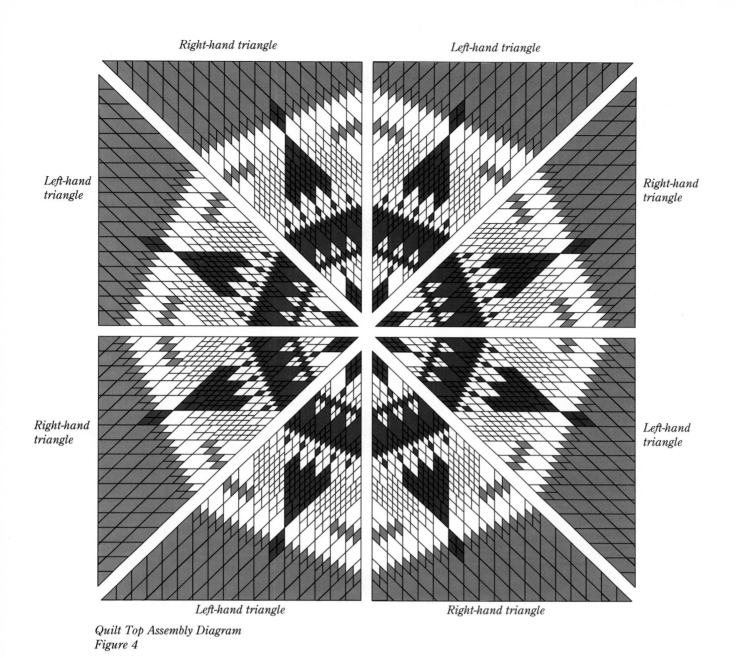

Right-hand triangle

Left-hand triangle

Left-hand triangle

Right-hand triangle

Left-hand triangle

Left-hand triangle

Right-hand triangle

Right-hand triangle

Quilt Top Assembly Diagram
Figure 4

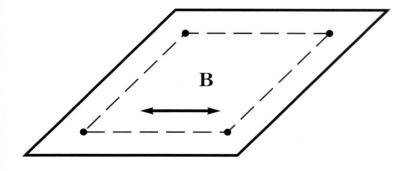

B

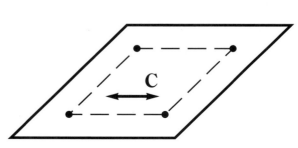

C

Sugar River Piecemakers
NEW GLARUS, WISCONSIN

Connie Gehin, Linda Geoffey, Barb Hoesly, Marietha Jelle, Judi Kane, Doris Klassly, Lennys Luchsinger, Diana Nelstad, Grace Notter, Melinda Notter, Carol Nyland, Agnes Rhyner, Norma Schenkel, Louise Schiese, Lorraine Schumacher, Dawn Slotten, Heather Slotten, Eleanor Smith, Lori Sutherland, Viola Trottman, Maryon Wand, Susie Wetherington.

Although the Sugar River Piecemakers was organized only in 1992, its impressive list of community activities is worthy of a much older group. According to Dawn Slotten, the Piecemakers' organizer, the guild spends much of its time together making baby quilts to contribute to local women's shelters. "We make tiny quilts for our hospital, too, sized to fit the incubators for babies in neonatal intensive care," Dawn says.

Some of the Piecemakers are also active in Habitat for Humanity, a nonprofit group that uses volunteer labor to build affordable houses for low-income families. As a result of their involvement, the guild completes a quilt for the new owners of each Habitat for Humanity house built in Green County. "It's important for people to feel that they have something to call their own," Dawn says. "Quilting is our way of passing that ownership on to people less fortunate than ourselves."

Richard's Star
1993

Richard's Star was designed by one of the members of the Sugar River Piecemakers, Judi Kane, as a raffle quilt to help the group raise money for its community outreach efforts. Because the quilt was to be made by women with varying degrees of quilting skill, Judi created an easily pieced pattern similar to the traditional Jacob's Ladder. The design had no name at that point; the members simply called it "the raffle quilt" or "the star quilt." Then Judi, pregnant with her first child, became very ill, and her son was born almost four months early. During his fight for life in the intensive care nursery, the Piecemakers voted to name the quilt design in honor of Judi's child, Richard.

It is because of Richard's difficult start in life that the Piecemakers have included the local hospital in their baby quilt donations. "We're just so glad that Judi and Richard are doing all right," Dawn says. "Maybe these quilts can give a little comfort to another tiny baby who needs it."

Dark blue print
2 (6½" x 75½") outer borders
2 (6½" x 99½") outer borders
192 A
Blue solid
192 A
Navy solid
2 (2" x 72½") inner borders
2 (2" x 96½") inner borders
4 (6½") corner squares

Quilt Top Assembly
1. Referring to Block Assembly Diagram, join 4 dark blue print As, 4 blue solid As, 2 light blue print Bs, and 2 mauve solid Bs to make 1 block. Repeat to make 48 blocks.

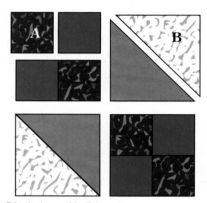

Block Assembly Diagram

2. Referring to Quilt Top Assembly Diagram for placement, join blocks in 8 rows of 6 blocks each. Join rows.

3. To make inner border, join 2" x 96½" navy solid border strips to sides of quilt top. Join 1 mauve solid C to each end of 1 (2" x 72½") navy solid border strip to make top border; repeat to make bottom border. Join to top and bottom of quilt top, butting corners.

4. To make outer border, join 6½" x 99½" dark blue print border strips to sides of quilt top. Join 1 navy solid corner square to each end of 1 (6½" x 75½") dark blue print border strip to make top border; repeat to make bottom border. Join to top and bottom of quilt top, butting corners.

Quilting
Quilt each seam in-the-ditch, or quilt as desired.

Finished Edges
Bind with bias binding made from navy.

Richard's Star

Finished Quilt Size
87" x 111"

Number of Blocks and Finished Size
48 blocks	12" x 12"

Fabric Requirements
Light blue print	1¾ yards
Mauve solid	1¾ yards
Dark blue print	3½ yards
Blue solid	1¾ yards
Navy solid	2¾ yards
Backing	8 yards
Navy solid for bias binding	1 yard

Pieces to Cut
Light blue print
96 B
Mauve solid
96 B
4 C

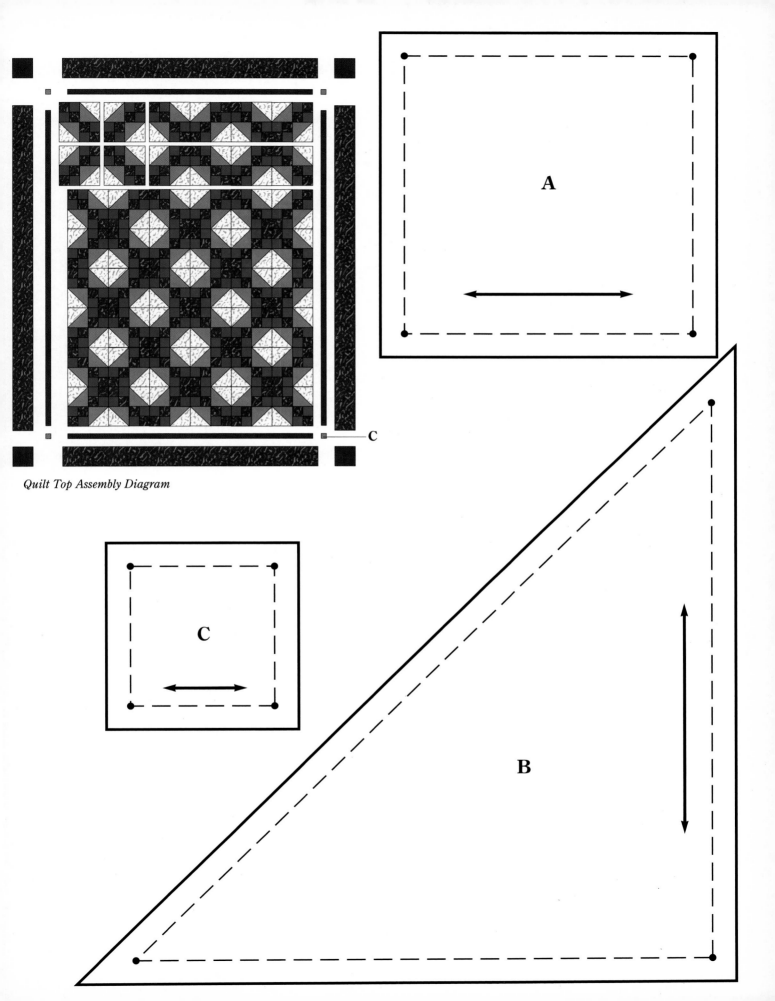

Quilt Top Assembly Diagram

A

B

C

Wenonah Depot Quilters
WENONAH, NEW JERSEY

Front row (L to R): Joan Baranek, Lea Wang, Jeanne Hagerman, Charla Newland. Second row (L to R): Cynthia Herrera, Joyce Maher, Renie Levecchia, Ruth Alkons, Nikki Agnew, Edna Schuchard. Third row (L to R): Diane Mickel, Eleanor Davis, Dorothy Heritage, Jean Boddingham, Judy Thompson, Nancy Smith, Nancy Wescott, Hilda Burke.

Wenonah, New Jersey, is a small community located about 10 miles south of Philadelphia. Many of the 30 women who now make up the Wenonah Depot Quilters met as members of Philadelphia-area guilds. Although these larger guilds filled a need in their quilting worlds, they found that they wanted the intimacy of a smaller group that could spend more time quilting. In 1991, they began holding meetings in the restored train depot that serves as Wenonah's community center, and the Wenonah Depot Quilters were born.

"We have no dues and no officers," says Renie Levecchia, one of the founding members. "But we do have fun!"

Cottages in the Snow
1992

Cottages in the Snow is the result of a Friendship Block exchange among the members of the Wenonah Depot Quilters. Each month, one member chooses a pattern and passes out pattern pieces and instructions to the others. The completed blocks, each one signed by its maker, are returned to her the following month, and another member passes out a new pattern.

In addition to the pattern for *Cottages in the Snow*, which was based on a block from the 1992 *Time and Seasons* calendar published by the Piecemakers Country Store in Costa Mesa, California, Renie also provided a variety of blue prints for the background fabric. "I told my friends to have fun!" she says. "They could add whatever they wanted to the block to personalize it. Some added chimneys, bird feeders, snowmen, and mailboxes. Some of the trees became Christmas trees, with sequins, beads, and fabric paint. When the blocks were returned to me, it was like Christmas!"

Cottages in the Snow

Finished Quilt Size
98" x 98"

Number of Blocks and Finished Size
25 blocks   14" x 14"

Fabric Requirements
Blue print	3 yards
White solid	4¾ yards
Red solid	¾ yard
Assorted red prints	1¼ yards
Assorted blue prints	5¼ yards
Assorted yellow prints	½ yard
Assorted green prints	1½ yards
Assorted gray or brown prints	⅔ yard
Backing	8⅔ yards
Blue print for bias binding	1 yard
Black embroidery floss	
Red embroidery floss	

Pieces to Cut
Blue print
  2 (6½" x 98½") outer borders
  2 (6½" x 86½") outer borders
  4 N

White solid
  2 (2½" x 82½") inner borders
  2 (2½" x 78½") inner borders
  4 (2½" x 78½") sashing strips
  20 (2½" x 14½") sashing strips
  25 D
  25 K
  25 L
  164 N
Red solid
  160 N
Assorted red prints
  25 C
Assorted blue prints
  25 (14½") background squares
Assorted yellow prints
  50 E
  25 F
  25 G
  25 H
  25 I
  25 M
Assorted green prints
  25 A
Assorted gray or brown prints
  25 B
  25 J

Quilt Top Assembly

1. Following Appliqué Placement Diagram, appliqué 1 A, 1 B, 1 C, 1 D, 2 Es, 1 F, 1 G, 1 H, 1 I, 1 J, 1 K, 1 L, and 1 M to 1 background square in alphabetical order. Using 2 strands of black embroidery floss, outline-stitch pane lines on windows E, F, G, H, and I. Using 3 strands of red embroidery floss, satin-stitch heart doorknob to complete 1 block. Repeat to make 25 blocks.

2. Join 5 blocks and 4 (2½" x 14½") white sashing strips to make 1 row. Repeat to make 5 rows. Join rows using 2½" x 78½" white sashing strips.

3. To make top pieced border, join 38 red Ns and 38 white Ns in red/white pairs to form squares; join squares, orienting triangles as shown in photograph. Join 1 (2½" x 78½") white inner border to red side of pieced border as shown in photograph. Repeat to make bottom border. Join to top and bottom of quilt.

4. To make 1 side pieced border, join 42 red Ns and 42 white Ns in red/white pairs. Join 2 white Ns and 2 blue print Ns in white/blue pairs. Join 40 red/white squares, orienting triangles as shown in photograph. Join 1 (2½" x 82½") white inner border to red side of pieced border. Join 1 red/white square to 1 white/blue square, orienting triangles as shown in photograph; join to 1 end of pieced border. Repeat to join remaining red/white and white/blue squares to other end of pieced border.

5. Repeat Step 4 to make second side pieced border. Join side borders to sides of quilt, butting corners.

6. Join 6½" x 86½" blue print borders to top and bottom of quilt. Join 6½" x 98½" blue print borders to sides of quilts, butting corners.

Quilting
Outline-quilt appliquéd figures and pieced borders. Quilt cable pattern (see "Resources") in sashing strips. Quilt diagonal lines, 2" apart, in white and blue print borders. Or quilt as desired.

Finished Edges
Bind with bias binding made from blue print fabric.

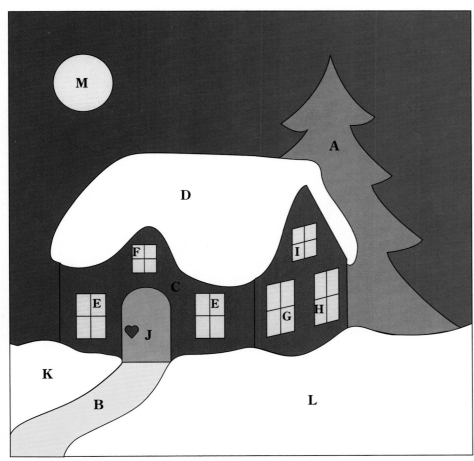

Appliqué Placement Diagram

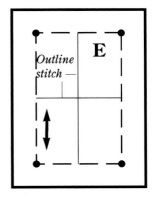

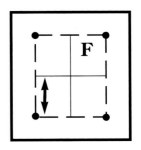

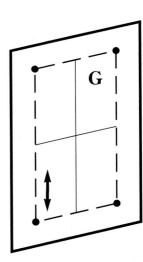

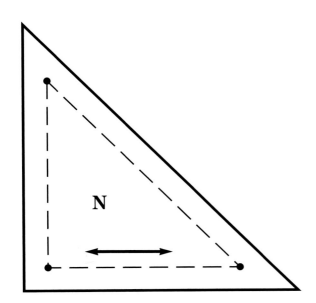

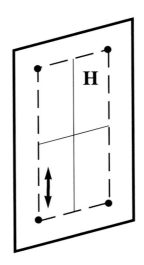

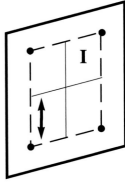

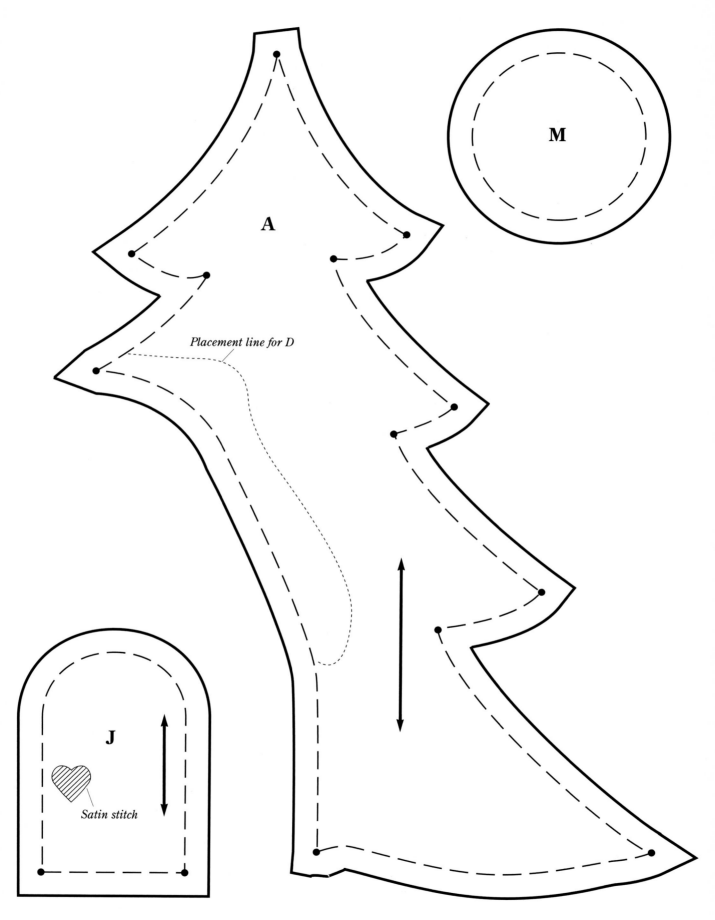

M

A

Placement line for D

J

Satin stitch

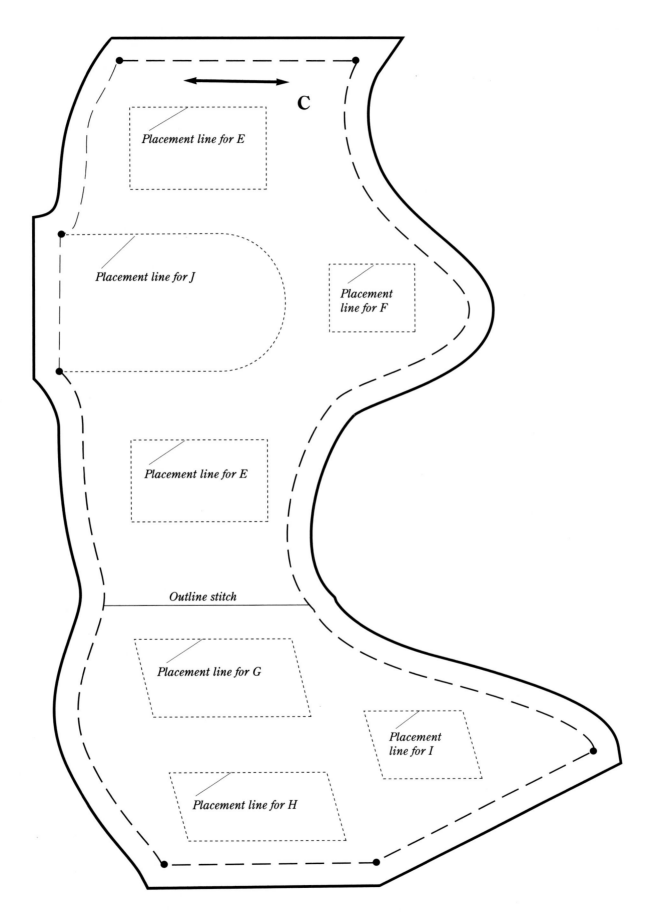

C

Placement line for E

Placement line for J

Placement
line for F

Placement line for E

Outline stitch

Placement line for G

Placement
line for I

Placement line for H

121

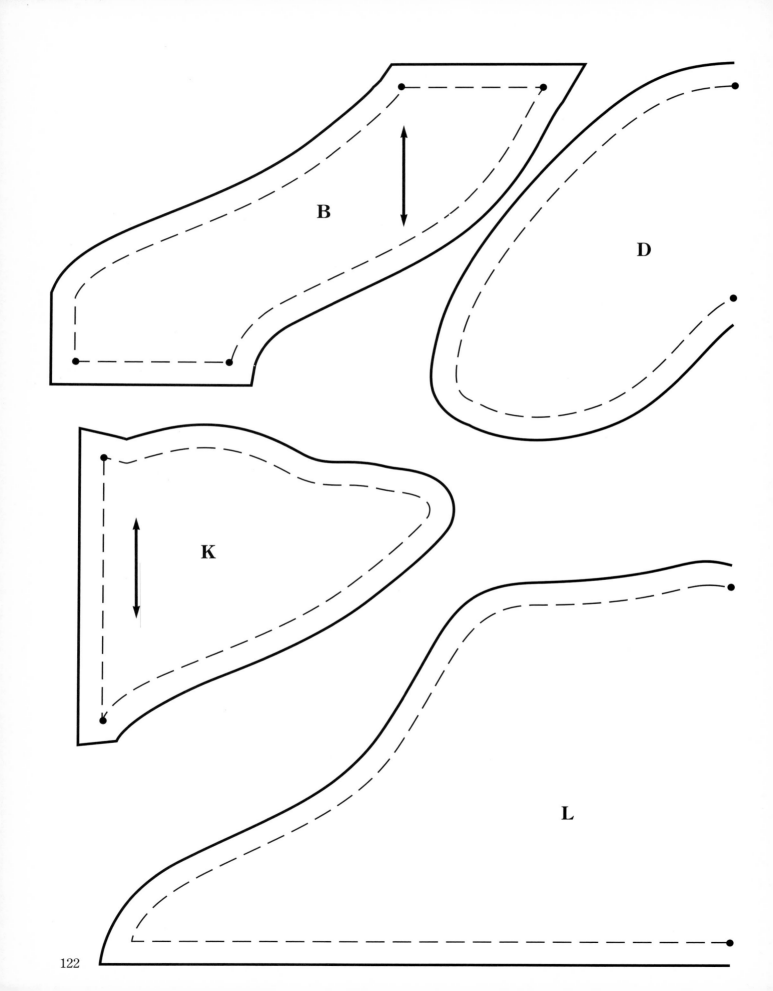

B

D

K

L

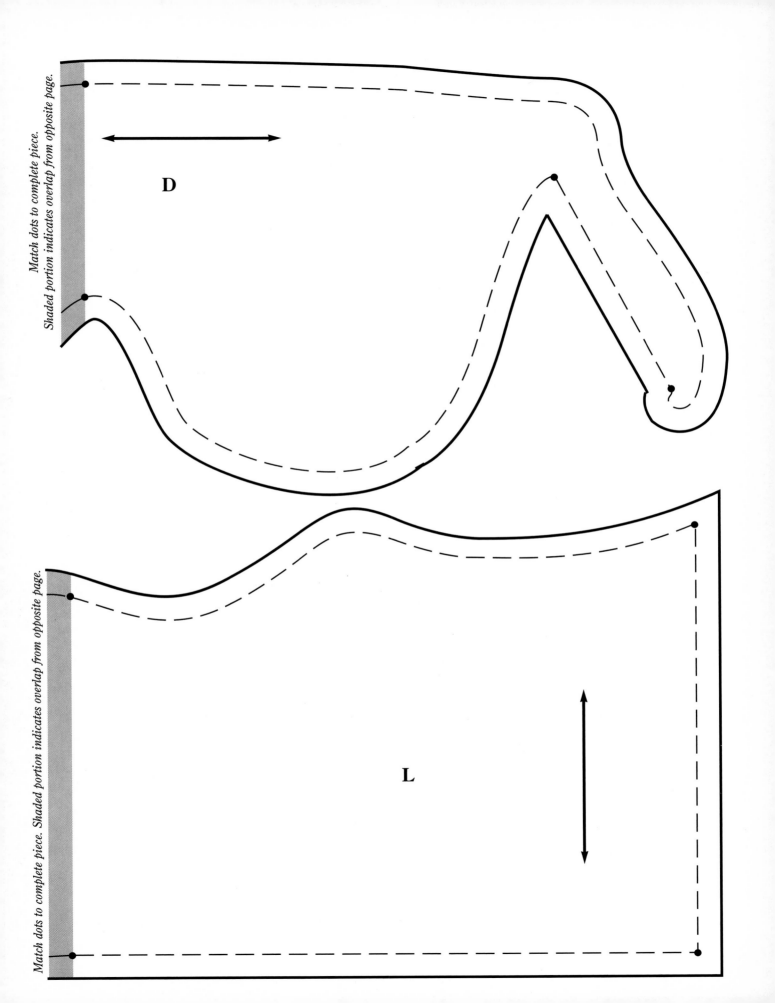

D

L

Barbara Abrelat and the Oxmoor House Quilters
BIRMINGHAM, ALABAMA

When Barbara Abrelat, a valued member of the Oxmoor House editorial staff, announced that she was moving to Atlanta, plans to make a farewell quilt for her quickly began to gel. The traditional Schoolhouse pattern was chosen to represent Oxmoor House, and a color scheme of red and muslin was chosen to help unify the blocks.

Because not all of the staffers who worked with Barbara felt comfortable making a quilt block, Susan Wright, the senior crafts editor, created the Schoolhouse stencil and arranged a stenciling work day in one of the photography studios to keep Barbara from finding out the secret too soon.

The completed blocks, each signed by the person who had made it, were presented to Barbara along with the best wishes of all her colleagues. But for Barbara, the challenge had only begun. She designed the setting and chose the teal print fabric to set off and unify the many red prints used in the blocks. And because there were others with whom she had worked at Oxmoor House who had not participated in making the quilt blocks, Barbara cut the signature panels from muslin and asked each of these special people to sign them.

After she completed the quilt, Barbara sent a photograph of it to all of us at Oxmoor House in her 1993 Christmas card. And we thought that you, our readers, would enjoy a little behind-the-scenes peek into why we feel that "there's no place like Oxmoor House."

There's No Place Like Oxmoor House
1993

Front row (L to R): Carol Newbill, Lelia Neil, Karen Brookshaw, Melissa Clark, Susan Cheatham, Barbara Abrelat.
Second row (L to R): Vicki Ingham, Susan Wright, Patricia Weaver, Margaret Allen Northen.
Third row (L to R): Cathy Corbett, Carol Hagood, Becky Brennan, Dondra Parham, Mary Kay Culpepper.
Fourth row (L to R): Wendy Wolford, Katie Stoddard, Linda Wright.

One of the blocks in Barbara's quilt reflects the whimsical sense of humor of its maker. Carol Hagood modified the Schoolhouse block so that the windows and roof of her house open to reveal a comical people print from Hoffman of California. The schoolhouse door was also altered to open to a special message.

125

Note that three of the Schoolhouse blocks in Barbara's quilt were made using various red scraps, and one block even has a red sky. Although we have given cutting instructions for making all Schoolhouse blocks alike, feel free to improvise, moving pieces among blocks to give your quilt a scrappy, impromptu feel.

There's No Place Like Oxmoor House

Finished Quilt Size
75" x 66"

Number of Blocks and Finished Size
18 Schoolhouse blocks   12" x 12"

Fabric Requirements
Muslin	2½ yards
Assorted red prints	2½ yards or 20 fat eighths
Teal print	1½ yards
Backing	4¼ yards
Red print for bias binding	1 yard

Pieces to Cut*
Muslin
2 (5½" x 10½") signature panels
14 (6½") squares for stenciling
36 A
18 C
18 D
18 D rev.
18 F
18 H
18 I
18 K
36 L
104 O

Assorted red prints
56 (1¼") sashing squares
36 B**
18 C**
18 E**
18 G**
36 I**
36 J**
36 L**
18 M**
52 N

Teal
15 (1½" x 12½") sashing strips
20 (1¼" x 12½") sashing strips
8 (1¼" x 7¼") sashing strips
56 (1¼" x 6½") sashing strips
28 P
8 Q
8 R
28 S

*No pattern pieces given for A, B, C, H, I, J, K, L, M, P, Q, R, or S. Use dimensions in Cutting Chart at right to rotary-cut these pieces. Or use dimensions to draw templates if you prefer.
**Cut 2 B, 1 C, 1 E, 1 G, 1 I, 2 J, 2 L, and 1 M from each print.

Quilt Top Assembly

1. To add signatures to muslin signature panels, cut 2 (5½" x 10½") pieces of freezer paper. If desired, draw lines on dull side of freezer paper to act as guidelines for signatures. Position 1 muslin panel, right side up, on shiny side of 1 sheet of freezer paper. Place press cloth over panel. Press to adhere fabric to paper, using dry iron set to "cotton." Using permanent, fine-point marking pen or laundry marker, add signatures to panel. Remove freezer paper. Place press cloth over panel and press to heat-set ink.

Repeat for second panel. Set signed panels aside.

2. Following instructions given in Quilt Smart on page 129, stencil 1 house on each 6½" muslin square.

3. Referring to Block Assembly diagrams, make 18 Schoolhouse blocks, 12 Goose Block 1s, and 4 Goose Block 2s. To complete 1 Signature Block, join 1 P to each short end of 1 signature panel. Join 1 S to each long end of panel, butting corners. Repeat to complete second Signature Block.

4. Referring to Quilt Top Assembly Diagram, join 4 Schoolhouse blocks and 3 (1½" x 12½") teal sashing strips to make 1 Row 1. Repeat to make 3 Row 1s. Join 2 Goose Block 1s (with "geese" facing toward center of quilt), 3 Schoolhouse blocks, and 3 (1½" x 12½") teal sashing strips to make 1 Row 2. Repeat to make second Row 2. Join rows as shown.

5. To make top border, join 3 stencilled house blocks, 2 Goose Block 1s, and 2 Goose Block 2s with teal sashing strips and red print sashing squares, as shown in Quilt Top Assembly Diagram. Make sure that geese point toward center of quilt. Repeat to make bottom border. Join borders to top and bottom of quilt.

To make 1 side border, join 4 stencilled house blocks, 2 Goose Block 1s, and 1 Signature Block with teal sashing strips and red print sashing squares, as shown in Quilt Top Assembly Diagram. Make sure that geese point toward center of quilt. Repeat to make second side border. Join borders to sides of quilt, butting corners.

Quilting
Quilt in-the-ditch around all seams, or quilt as desired.

Finished Edges
Bind with bias binding made from red print fabric.

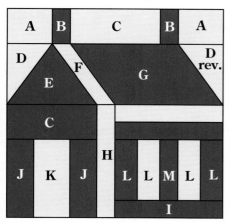

Schoolhouse Block—Make 18.

Goose Block 1—Make 12.

Goose Block 2—Make 4.

Signature Block—Make 2.

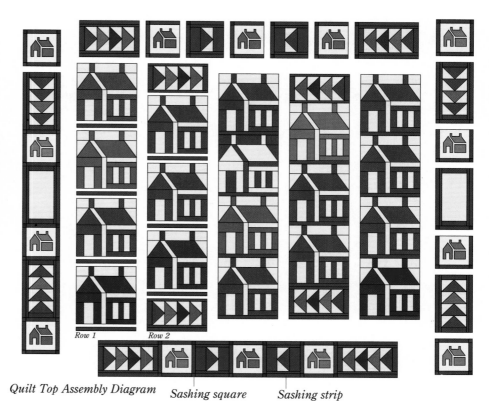

Quilt Top Assembly Diagram   *Sashing square*   *Sashing strip*

Piece	Size
(including seam allowances)	
A	2½" x 3"
B	1½" x 2½"
C	2½" x 5½"
H	1½" x 7"
I	1½" x 6½"
J	2" x 5"
K	2½" x 5"
L	1¾" x 4"
M	1½" x 4"
P	1½" x 5½"
Q	2⅝" x 5½"
R	1" x 7¼"
S	1" x 12½"

Cutting Chart

N

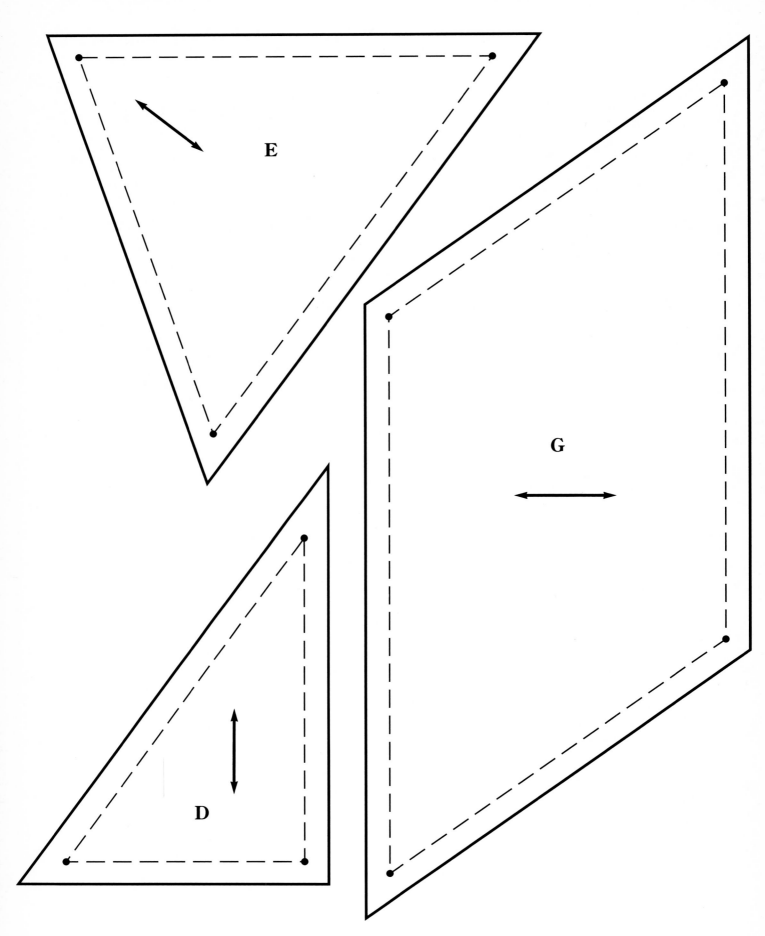

E

G

D

Stencil Pattern

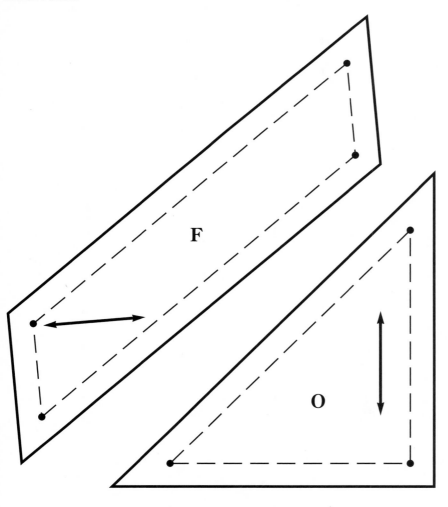

F

O

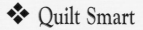

❖ Quilt Smart

Stenciling

Materials
Clear plastic template material
Masking tape
Soft lead pencil
Craft knife
Plate glass or other hard cutting
    surface
Transparent tape
Acrylic craft paint
Shallow dish
Blunt-bristle stencil brushes
Paper towels

Making Stencil
   Cut 8" square from clear plastic. Tape in place over stencil pattern at left and trace design using sharp pencil. Place on hard surface such as plate glass or cutting board. Using craft knife, cut out house elements shaded on pattern, keeping edges as smooth as possible. Patch miscuts with transparent tape.

Stenciling Design
   Pour small amount of paint into shallow dish. Dip end of stencil brush into paint and dab bristles on clean paper towels to blot excess paint. To ensure sharp outline, work with almost-dry brush.
   Tape stencil to right side of fabric. Working from outside of each cut area toward center, apply paint with tapping motion, straight up and down. When all cut areas have been painted, remove stencil and wipe clean with a wet paper towel. Clean stencils and brushes with soap and warm water.
   Allow stenciled design to dry. Using a medium-hot, dry iron and press cloth, press fabric to set paint.

DESIGNER GALLERY

Jane McGriff Herlong
BIRMINGHAM, ALABAMA

reelance graphic designer Jane Herlong has enjoyed needlework since a very early age. Her interest in quiltmaking was first sparked by a friendship quilt she received as a wedding gift. "When one of my friends was expecting her first child," Jane says, "I decided I wanted to make a baby quilt for her. So I asked another friend who enjoyed quilting to show me how to appliqué and piece." The result—Jane's first quilt—was *The Bug Quilt,* reflecting the child's father's occupation of entomology, the study of insects.

"All of my designs have been pictorial," Jane says, "and appliqué is the best way I have found to achieve a realistic portrayal. I also like adding embroidery—a technique I like to think of as 'drawing in slow motion'—because it brings the whole thing to life."

Zoo
1989

When Jane decided to make a quilt as a gift for her 7-year-old godson, she knew that the quilt should reflect Matthew's love of animals. "But," Jane says, "his mother warned me not to make it too 'cute' or 'babyish,' so I made my design realistic."

Despite the almost photographic appearance of the animals, the faces are made entirely from solid fabrics, skillfully appliquéd and embroidered.

The cobra's body encircling the border is cut from a printed fabric, with additional appliqué and embroidery forming the hood and face. *Zoo* was awarded Best of Show at the 1989 North Jefferson Quilters Guild annual quilt show.

Barbara Abrelat's experience as an illustrator has certainly influenced her work as a quiltmaker. She usually makes quilts from her own original designs, and she tailors each quilt to suit the person or event for whom it is intended. She likes to try something new with every quilt she makes, whether it is an unusual arrangement of colors and patterns, a technique she has not used before, or a design challenge waiting to be worked through.

Although she frequently employs machine piecing in her quiltmaking, Barbara prefers to quilt by hand. "I love to see the design come to life with dimension as the stitches are applied," she explains.

Barbara Abrelat
DECATUR, GEORGIA

City of Gold
1993

In celebration of the 1996 Olympic Summer Games, Barbara designed and made this marvelous quilt that captures the spirit of Atlanta.

"Atlanta's identification with the phoenix began with the city's rebirth after the fiery destruction of the Civil War," Barbara says. Her quilt, which portrays this image of triumph with the skyline of today's Atlanta in the background, is one of over 400 quilts made by Georgia quilters for the Atlanta Olympics. The flag bearer of each nation, as well as a representative of each nation's organizing committee, will take home one of these gift quilts as a slice of Americana and an example of Southern hospitality.

"The wings of the phoenix are spread to welcome the visitors from around the world," Barbara says. "This is such a personal way to participate in the Olympics—I wanted this to be a very special quilt."

Front row (L to R): Millie Berryhill, Diane Pina, Martha Garrison, Cheri Ruzich, Pat May, Diana Tatro. Middle row (L to R): Ruth Hilbers, Sheelah Thomas, Marlene Hall, Debra Luis, Shirley McElyea, Marty Zeleny, Mary Overton, Melanie Harman. Back row (L to R): Cindy Frey, Yvette Stark, Emily Olson, Carol Empey, Ila Shaw, Judy Hawkins, Sharon Easter, Ayce Kauffman.

Front row (L to R): Diane Leighton, Cooky Amarel, Peggy White. Middle row (L to R): Mahrnelle Finley, Nancy Trammel, Willie Williams, Coyla Hewitt, Rosemary Smiley, Ann Tutor-Marks. Back row (L to R): Marilee Churchill, Rebecca Chapin, Beryl Burtis, Elaine Latimer, Bette Kennedy, Shirley Taylor, Marjorie Zwald.

Valley Quilt Guild
YUBA CITY, CALIFORNIA

Till the Cows Come Home
1993

Cheri Ruzich, designer of *Till the Cows Come Home,* joined the Valley Quilt Guild in 1990. In 1991, Cheri was elected vice-president and Debra Luis president, and a close friendship developed during their two-year term in office. During that time, Cheri secretly spearheaded the effort to create a president's gift quilt for Debra—the first such quilt ever presented by the guild. Knowing that Debra and her husband, Mike, are dairy farmers, Cheri adapted a cow pattern by Ruth Seeley-Scheel called "Udderly Inviting" for the focal point of Debra's quilt, adding borders of barns and Lemoyne Stars in Debra's favorite colors.

Till the Cows Come Home won First Place–Large Quilts and Best of Show at the 1993 Valley Quilt Guild Show and the Best of Category Award at the 1993 Yuba Sutter Fair. And in June of 1994, it won both Best of Show and Best of Theme at the San Francisco Quilt Guild's Show held—where else?—at the Cow Palace. And the theme of the San Francisco Guild's show was most appropriate: "Udderly Fantastic."

J udith Hindall, whose quilt *Starlight Nights–Garden Delights* appears in the "Quilts Across America" chapter, has only been making quilts for three years. She views her quiltmaking as an opportunity to spend time with her husband. "I am a one-stitch-at-a-time quilter," Judy says. "I work in my favorite chair in the living room while my husband watches television. This is something I can do while I'm with my husband, so we can enjoy our evenings together." She also takes her quilting with her to work, where she finds relaxation by stitching during her lunch hour.

"I prefer hand piecing," Judy says, "but I have learned to machine-piece to save time. The people I have met at guilds, workshops, and retreats have given me such a wealth of ideas that I'll never live long enough to make them all!"

Judith Hindall
STOW, OHIO

Moonbeam's Daydreams
1993

Judy attended a quilter's retreat where she was challenged to come up with an original quilt design. The guidelines stated that the quilt must feature black fabric with stars and a three-dimensional element. To meet this challenge, she not only designed this unusual quilt, but she also painted her own fabric to create the realistic look of a tabby cat. Referring to a picture of a real cat, Judy painted dark tan stripes on a pale tan background and then heat-set her design. She inserted extra batting into Moonbeam's body to make him more dimensional.

Her work is so convincing that her real cat was jealous of Moonbeam! Perhaps other quilters were jealous as well—the quilt took first place in the 1993 Keep Us in Stitches guild show in Independence, Ohio. But perhaps the most important prize this quilt has won is Judy's affection; she says, "I like this piece a lot and always smile when I look at it."

Linda Steider
WHITE SALMON, WASHINGTON

Raven Marries Fog Woman
1992

Linda based this quilt on a legend of the Haida-Tlingit people, native to the Queen Charlotte Islands off the coast of Washington State. "I was so moved by the legend that the image appeared over and over while I worked on other projects," Linda says. "I then searched and searched for the right fabrics and yarns, especially for Fog Woman's hair." She also used hand-dyed fabrics and netting to create the underwater effect at the bottom of the quilt, as well as the rolling sky at the top. There are salmon positioned at various depths in the sea, over and under the layers of "water" netting.

Raven is composed primarily of UltraSuede, with bits of satin and velveteen. Fog Woman is a collection of unravelled metallic thread and ribbon floss, as well as bits and pieces of lamé, yarn, strips of UltraSuede, and rows of beading. The quilt is marvelously textured and glistens from all angles. "As each piece fell into place, I could see what to do with the next one!" Linda says. "It was an exhilarating experience."

You might say Linda Steider has a passion—a passion for quilting, that is. "I don't think I could live or breathe without it!" she says. She sometimes quilts for 16 hours a day and has made approximately 100 quilts in her 16 years of experience. That's a quilt every two months!

Linda speaks fondly of her relationship with her craft. Through quilting, she went from being a shy, quiet person to becoming the president of a local quiltmaker's organization and director of The Columbia Stitchery Guild. "I have experienced great personal growth through quilting," she says. "It has even led me to further my education. The more I learn, the more I realize how much I don't know and want to learn!" Linda also teaches quilting to both adults and children, to encourage others to learn the art that has given her so much.

Linda added this embroidered scroll under Raven's wing to help tell the tale of Raven and Fog Woman.

136

Susan Vernon's job as a free-lance artist has been influenced by her recently acquired hobby, quiltmaking. "Quilting has added another dimension to my love of design," she says. "It employs color and form in a three-dimensional state." She uses only original designs, often drafting ideas from her own paintings, drawings, and photographs. "Pictorial quilts are particularly satisfying because they allow the viewer to experience a 'story' created by her own imagination."

Susan is currently designing quilted garments and fabric-and-clay dolls and is illustrating a children's book being written by her daughter. Amazingly, she still finds time to design and create quilts, as well as serve as president of the East Cobb Quilter's Guild.

Susan P. Vernon
ROSWELL, GEORGIA

Soaring
1992

Susan's son shared with her some photographs he had taken of a hot-air balloon race over the New Mexico desert. "It was breathtaking!" she exclaims. "I immediately saw this as a quilt, even though I had never made one." Susan used other photographs to create the aerial view below the balloons.

"*Soaring* was designed without a true perspective," she says, "but more of a child-like interpretation of a flight over the treetops." This treatment conveys the youthful excitement of such a balloon ride. Susan blended fabrics of varying weights to add depth to her quilt, such as heavy drapery fabric for the baskets and brighter, lighter material for the actual balloons. The sheep, horses, and other animals are crafted from bits of felt. The balloon motif crosses the lower border to further enhance the dimensional impact of the quilt.

"Quiltmaking satisfies all my creative needs. It provides the joys and challenges of working in a medium I love."

Jonathan Shannon
BELVEDERE, CALIFORNIA

Although he has been making quilts only since 1988, Jonathan Shannon, an artist by training, is thoroughly familiar with fiber and design. A graduate of UCLA, Jonathan lived in London during the mid-1960s, at the time of "mod fashion" and the "Carnaby Street look," and brought that excitement to Los Angeles when he returned in 1968. He opened a tiny shop in Hollywood with a stock of 35 men's shirts that he had designed, hoping that they would sell well enough to justify the plunge. "Fortunately," Jonathan says, "the head-quarters of Capitol Records was around the corner, and every major rock-and-roll star of that era walked by the shop. I sold out within two days, and by the end of the week I had a staff of four." He soon began designing women's clothing as well, for a client list that included actresses Ann-Margret, Raquel Welch, and Elizabeth Taylor.

In 1988, an old copy of *Americana* magazine showing quilts on the cover caught Jonathan's eye. He realized at once that, with his background in textiles, quiltmaking was well within his reach. "I was excited to discover that quilts are not only for beds," Jonathan says, "but can also be very personal statements of artistic creation."

Canciones de mi Padre
1988

This dynamic design, which won first place in the 1989 "Quilting by the Lake" contest in Cazenovia, New York, was Jonathan Shannon's first quilt. To reflect the musical theme of the contest, Jonathan drew upon the liveliness and vivacity of Linda Ronstadt's recording of traditional Mexican music, *Canciones de mi Padre* ("Songs of My Father"), in his design. "The central circular shape represents the swirling skirts of dancers at a fiesta," Jonathan says. "The black and white inner border recalls the black and white outfits often worn by Mexican musicians, and the outer border is the traditional Mexican Cross block."

In addition to its first-place ribbon at Cazenovia, *Canciones de mi Padre* won Best First Quilt at the Marin County Needle Arts Show in San Rafael, California.

QUILT SMART WORKSHOP
A Guide to Quiltmaking

Preparing Fabric

Before cutting out any pieces, be sure to wash and dry your fabric to preshrink it. All-cotton fabrics may need to be pressed before cutting. Trim selvages from the fabric before you cut your pieces.

Making Templates

Before you can make one of the quilts in this book, you must make templates from the printed pattern pieces given. Quilters have used many materials to make templates, including cardboard and sandpaper. Transparent template plastic, available at craft supply and quilt shops, is durable, see-through, and easy to use.

To make templates using plastic, place the plastic sheet on the printed page and trace the pattern piece, using a laundry marker or permanent fine-tip marking pen. For machine piecing, trace along the outside solid (cutting) line. For hand piecing, trace along the inside broken (stitching) line. Cut out the template along the traced line. Label each template with the pattern name, letter, grain line arrow, and match points (corner dots).

To make window templates for use in cutting specific motifs from print fabric, see Quilt Smart on page 44 (*Starlight Nights-Garden Delights*).

Marking and Cutting Fabric

Place the template facedown on the wrong side of the fabric and mark around the template with a sharp pencil. Move the template (see next two paragraphs) and continue marking pieces; mark several before you stop to cut.

If you will be piecing your quilt by machine, the pencil lines represent the cutting lines. Leave about ¼" between pieces as you mark. Cut along the marked lines.

For hand piecing, the pencil lines are the seam lines. Leave at least ¾" between marked lines for seam allowances. Add ¼" seam allowance around each piece as you cut. Mark match points (corner dots) on each piece.

Hand Piecing

To hand piece, place two fabric pieces together with right sides facing. Insert a pin in each match point of the top piece. Stick the pin through both pieces and check to be sure that it pierces the match point on the bottom piece (Figure 1). Adjust the pieces if necessary to align the match points. (The raw edges of the two

pieces may not be exactly aligned.) Pin the pieces securely together.

Sew with a running stitch of 8 to 10 stitches per inch. Checking your stitching as you go to be sure that you are stitching in the seam line of both pieces, sew from match point to match point. To make sharp corners, begin and end the stitching exactly at the match point; do not stitch into the seam allowances. When joining units where several seams come together, do not sew over seam allowances; sew through them at the point where all seam lines meet (Figure 2).

Always press both seam allowances to one side. Pressing the seam open, as in dressmaking, may leave gaps between the stitches through which quilt batting may beard. Press seam allowances toward the darker fabric whenever you can. When four or more seams meet at one point, such as at the corner of a block, press all the seams in a "swirl" in the same direction to reduce bulk (Figure 3).

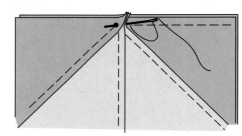

1—*Aligning Match Points*

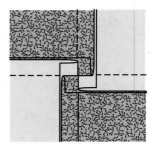

2—*Joining Units*

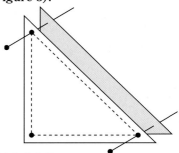

3—*Pressing Intersecting Seams*

Machine Piecing

To machine piece, place two fabric pieces together with right sides facing. Align match points as described under "Hand Piecing" and pin the pieces together securely.

Set your stitch length at 12 to 15 stitches per inch. At this setting, you will not need to backstitch to lock seam beginnings and ends. Use a presser foot that gives a perfect ¼" seam allowance, or measure ¼" from the sewing machine needle and mark that point on the presser foot with nail polish or masking tape.

Chain-piece sections, stitching edge to edge, to save time when sewing similar sets of pieces (Figure 4). Join the first two pieces as usual. At the end of the seam, do not backstitch, cut the thread, or lift the presser foot. Instead, sew a few stitches off the fabric. Place the next two pieces and continue stitching. Keep sewing until all the sets are joined. Then cut the sets apart.

Press seam allowances toward the darker fabric. When you join blocks or rows, press the seam allowances of the top piece in one direction and the seam allowances of the bottom piece in the opposite direction to help ensure that the seams will lie flat (Figure 5).

For help with piecing curves, see Quilt Smart on page 12 (*Flying Under Radar*) and page 27 (*Whispering Leaves*). For help with set-in seams, see Quilt Smart on page 17 (*Cool and Bold*).

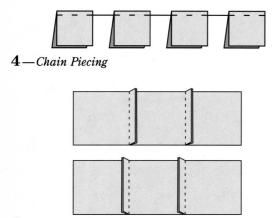

4—*Chain Piecing*

5—*Pressing Seams for Machine Piecing*

Hand Appliqué

Hand appliqué is the best way to achieve the look of traditional appliqué. However, using freezer paper, which is sold in grocery stores, can save a lot of time because it eliminates the need for hand basting the seam allowances.

Make templates without seam allowances. Trace the template onto the *dull* side of the freezer paper and cut the paper on the marked line. Make a freezer paper shape for each piece to be appliquéd. Pin the freezer paper shape, with its *shiny side up,* to the *wrong side* of your fabric. Following the paper shape and adding a scant ¼" seam allowance, cut out the fabric piece. Do not remove the pins. Using the tip of a hot, dry iron, press the seam allowance to the shiny side of the freezer paper. Be careful not to touch the shiny side of the freezer paper with the iron. Remove the pins.

Pin the appliqué shape in place on the background fabric. Use one strand of sewing thread in a color to match the appliqué shape. Using a very small slipstitch (Figure 6) or blindstitch (Figure 7), appliqué the shape to the background fabric.

After your stitching is complete, cut away the background fabric behind the appliqué shape, leaving ¼" seam allowance. Separate the freezer paper from the fabric with your fingernail and pull gently to remove it.

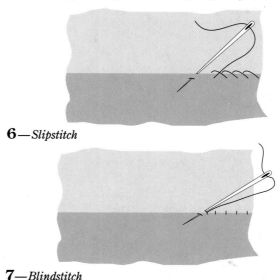

6—*Slipstitch*

7—*Blindstitch*

Mitering Borders

Mitered borders take a little extra care to construct. First, measure your quilt. Cut two border strips to fit the shorter of two opposite sides, plus the width of the border plus 2". Now center the measurement for the shorter side on one border strip and place a pin at each end of the measurement. Match the pins on the border strip to the corners of the longer side of the quilt. Join the border strip to the quilt, easing the quilt to fit between the pins and stopping ¼" from each corner of the quilt (Figure 8). Join the remaining cut strip to the opposite end of the quilt. Cut and join the remaining borders in the same manner. Press seams to one side. Follow Figures 9 and 10 to miter corners.

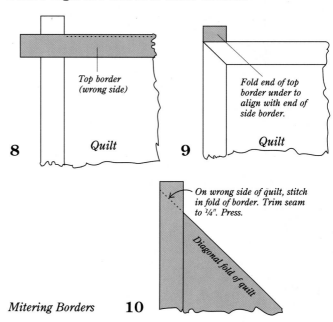

Top border (wrong side)

Fold end of top border under to align with end of side border.

8   *Quilt*   **9**   *Quilt*

On wrong side of quilt, stitch in fold of border. Trim seam to ¼". Press.

Diagonal fold of quilt

Mitering Borders   **10**

Marking Your Quilt Top

After the quilt top is completed, it should be thoroughly pressed and then marked with quilting designs. The most popular methods for marking use stencils or templates. Both can be purchased, or you can make your own. Use a silver quilter's pencil for marking light to medium fabrics and a white artist's pencil on dark fabrics. Lightly mark the quilt top with your chosen quilting designs.

Making a Backing

While some fabric and quilt shops sell 90" and 108" widths of backing fabric, the instructions in *Great American Quilts* give backing yardage based on 45"-wide fabric. When using 45"-wide fabric, all quilts wider than 42" will require a pieced backing. For quilts whose width measures between 42" and 80", purchase an amount of fabric equal to two times the desired length of the unfinished quilt backing. (The unfinished quilt backing should be at least 3" larger on all sides than the quilt top.)

The backing fabric should be of a type and color that is compatible with the quilt top. Percale sheets are not recommended because they are tightly woven and difficult to hand-quilt through.

A pieced backing for a bed quilt should have three panels. The three-panel backing is recommended because it tends to wear better and lie flatter than the two-panel type, the center seam of which often makes a ridge down the center of the quilt. Begin by cutting the fabric in half widthwise (Figure 11). Open the two lengths and stack them, with right sides facing and selvages aligned. Stitch along both selvage edges to create a tube of fabric (Figure 12). Cut down the center of the top layer of fabric *only* and open the fabric flat (Figure 13).

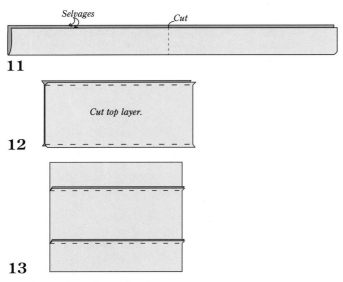

11

12

13

Making a Three-Panel Backing

Layering and Basting

Prepare a working surface to spread out the quilt. Place the backing on the working surface right side down. Unfold the batting and place it on top of the backing. Smooth any wrinkles or lumps in the batting.

Lay the quilt top right side up on top of the batting and backing. Make sure the backing and quilt top are aligned. Knot a long strand of sewing thread and use a darning needle for basting. Begin basting in the center of your quilt and baste out toward the edges. The stitches should cover an ample amount of the quilt so that the quilt layers do not shift during quilting. Inadequate basting can result in puckers and folds on the back and front of the quilt.

Hand Quilting

Hand quilting can be done with the quilt in a hoop or in a floor frame. It is best to start quilting in the middle of your quilt and work out toward the edges.

Most quilters use a very thin, short needle called a "between." Betweens are available in sizes 7 to 12, with 7 being the longest and 12 the shortest. If you are a beginning quilter, try a size 7 or 8. Because betweens are so much shorter than other hand-sewing needles, they may feel awkward at first. As your skill increases, try switching to a smaller needle to help you make smaller stitches.

Quilting thread, heavier and stronger than ordinary sewing thread, is available in a wide variety of colors. But if color matching is critical and you can't find the color you need, you may substitute cotton sewing thread. We suggest you coat it with beeswax before quilting to prevent it from tangling and knotting.

To begin, thread your needle with an 18" to 24" length and make a small knot at one end. Insert the needle into the top of the quilt approximately ½" from the point you want to begin quilting. Do not take the needle through all three layers, but stop it in the batting and bring it up through the quilt top again at your starting point. Tug gently on the thread to pop the knot through the quilt top into the batting. This anchors the thread without an unsightly knot showing on the back. With your non-sewing hand underneath the quilt, insert the needle with the point straight down in the quilt about 1/16" from the starting point. With your underneath finger, feel for the point as the needle comes through the backing (Figure 14). Place the thumb of your sewing hand approximately ½" ahead of your needle. At the moment you feel the needle touch your underneath finger, push the fabric up from below as you rock the needle down to a nearly horizontal position. Using the thumb of your sewing hand in conjunction with the underneath hand, pinch a little hill in the fabric and push the tip of the needle back through the quilt top (Figure 15).

Now either push the needle all the way through to complete one stitch or rock the needle again to an upright position on its point to take another stitch. Take no more than a quarter-needleful of stitches before pulling the needle through.

When you have about 6" of thread remaining, you must end the old thread securely and invisibly. Carefully tie a knot in the thread, flat against the surface of the fabric. Pop the knot through the top as you did when beginning the line of quilting. Clip the thread, rethread your needle, and continue quilting.